Priscilla

THE GUIDE TO HOME DECORATING

Indian Style

To Rick & Kathleen,

Such a pleasure to meet
you! Please enjoy the read.

Priscilla
Feb. 19, 2013

THE GUIDE TO HOME DECORATING

Indian Style

PRISCILLA KOHUTEK

MAPIN PUBLISHING PVT. LTD.

First published in 2001 by
Mapin Publishing Pvt. Ltd.
31 Somnath Road, Usmanpura
Ahmedabad 380013 INDIA
email: mapinpub@icenet.net
www.mapinpub.com

in association with
Grantha Corporation
80 Cliffedgeway
Middletown, NJ 07701 USA

Distributed in North America by
Antique Collectors' Club
Market Street Industrial Park
Wappingers' Falls, NY 12590 USA
Tel: 800-252-5231 Fax: 845-297-0068
email: info@antiquecc.com
www.antiquecc.com

Distributed in UK and Europe by
Art Books International
1 Stewart's Court, 220 Stewart's Road
London SW8 4UD
Tel: (020) 7720 1503 Fax: 7720 3158
email: stanley@art-bks.com

Distributed in Asia (except South Asia) by
Hemisphere Publication Services
240 Macpherson Road
#08-01 Pines Industrial Building
Singapore 348574
Tel: 65-741-5166 • Fax: 65-742-9356
email: info@hemisphere.com.sg

ISBN: 1-890206-21-0 (Grantha)
ISBN: 81-85822-70-0 (Mapin)
LC: 99-76982

Text styling by Priscilla Kohutek
Edited by Priscilla Kohutek, Toni Slifer and Mallika Sarabhai
Consulting Editor: Krishan Kak
Designed by Priscilla Kohutek and Pallon Daruwala
Processed by Reproscan, Mumbai
Printed by Tien Wah Press, Singapore

To my husband,
Eddie

Acknowledgements

To all those who made *The Guide to Home Decorating Indian Style* possible, I extend my sincere thanks and appreciation.

To my illustrator Sheryl Perry for her beautiful watercolour renderings.

To photographers Peter Mealin and especially Pallon Daruwala who shot the bulk of the photos for this book.

To Arlette Phanning for transcribing my radio tapes.

To Melinda Alexander, Maureen Berlin, Rosalie Chidwick, May Kottukapally-Demann, Elaine Ghosh, Joan Griffes, Simran Gupta, Gill Hough, Robert Mathis, Diane Moore, Anita Nair, Carol Ratcliff, and Yvette for opening their lovely homes to the prying lenses of the cameras.

To our wonderful daughter, Kathy McCormick, and dear friends Beverly Cooper, Toni Slifer and Michael Wickman for their early and continuing support.

To all the people at Mapin Publishing Pvt. Ltd. who made this book a reality.

Thank you.

C O N T

CHAPTER 1

Welcome...

INTRODUCTION

You are about to begin a journey into the exciting world of home decorating, where the adventures along the way are half the fun. While there are many road maps to guide you, there is only one hard and fast rule of the road: go slowly! Take time to enjoy giving your home an attractive, comfortable atmosphere, free of the worldly stress that bombards us on a daily basis — a haven of peace and quiet where the family goes to get rejuvenated. When the project is done with loving care to suit the ever-changing needs of those who live there, the toil and trouble are well worth the effort, and you have achieved the goal of creating a real *home*.

This task is not without challenges and some difficulties. Although the old adage that the things worth having are worth working for is applicable, this book is designed to make the job easier. The following chapters are full of techniques for starting projects and seeing them come to fruition through applying practical and economical methods.

GETTING STARTED

Whether you are doing up your whole place or redecorating a single room, the starting point is thinking about the total concept — the general look and feeling you're after. Having decided that, mentally work your way from room to room so the decor will flow throughout your home. When the work actually begins, don't try to take on the whole house at once — focus on one thing at a time. By completely doing up a whole room before you move on, you'll get a feeling of accomplishment and see the results much quicker than if you hop around doing a little bit here and there.

Choose the room that you want to do up first by deciding which one is bugging you the most. For example, let's say it's the kitchen. By job description, most home-makers spend a good deal of time in the kitchen, so it should have a friendly and inviting feeling. But, if it's such a mess you hate to go in there, that's the room to tackle first.

Undertake the project when you're at your best. Never start off when you are tired or pre-occupied with something else. If you're a morning person, that's the right time for you. If you're a night owl, then go to it when everybody else has gone to bed.

Survey the territory with a very critical eye. Don't get hung up on the things you can't change like the size of the room. Concentrate on working with the elements as they are — think about what is possible.❧

Q. What is a practical way to approach a decorating project?

A. Review *Getting Started* and make some notes about where you want to start. Then ask yourself these questions about function and form:

What is the function of this room? (What will it be used for?)

How many people will be using this room? What are their combined needs?

Next, you must decide on the form of the room, which is how you want it to look and feel:

Do you like a warm, cosy environment, full of your favourite things or do you prefer cool, sleek interiors with uncluttered surfaces?

Do you adore antiques or hate them?

Do you like basic-looking rooms or do you go for a lot of fluff?

If you haven't got a clue about what you want or don't want, now is the time to educate yourself. Study every decorating magazine you can get your hands on, both local and foreign. This part of the project doesn't have to cost a bomb if you shop and swap with your friends. It works this way: go to the bookstores with a group of friends. Each person buys one magazine, and you trade off with one another.

Make file folders marked kitchens, bathrooms, bedrooms, living rooms, dining rooms. When you see a picture of something you like, tear out that page and put it into the appropriate file — this includes window treatments for each room, lighting, accessories, and appliances.

Every two to four weeks go through each file and throw out those pictures that no longer appeal to you. You should be constantly adding to and editing your files. After a while, a pattern will form, and you will be able to see in what direction you're leaning.

As you go through these exercises again and again, you will begin to have confidence in what you like and don't like. You are developing a sense of style and learning to trust yourself. Believe me, this takes time and effort. To this day, I constantly read magazines and religiously work on my files.

Q. Are there any shortcuts for redecorating just one room?

A. Not really. You must still go through the function and form exercises, study decorating books and magazines, and build your file. Then, take a good hard look at the things you have in the room to determine what you can use, what needs freshening up, and what goes in the garbage.

Tip: If ideas are hard to come by or you have trouble visualising, don't despair. Keep your decorating project simple and on a small scale until you get the hang of it.

Q. Where does one begin when faced with a completely empty room? I've decided on the furniture style, but I don't know how to coordinate everything. Should I pick the fabric for the upholstered pieces first and work from there, or should the floor and drapes be done first, or what?

A. When you are starting from scratch, start at the bottom and work your way up. Begin with the floor covering, select the furniture upholstery next, then do the window treatment, move on to wall hangings, and finish off with accessories.

Take the guesswork out of coordinating patterns and colours for upholstery and curtains with mix-and-match fabrics available at many of the local decorator shops. Borrow large samples, spread them around on the floor covering (bare, carpeted or area rug), and make your selection.

Start with the largest piece of furniture — in the bedroom that would be the bed; in the living room and family room /den it would probably be the sofa — and move on to the chairs, and so forth. Do up all of the upholstered pieces and place them in the room before you decide on the window treatment. Otherwise, you may end up with a busy, overpowering look.

Q. I'm a bachelor who will be moving into a large flat with my mother. Please give me some decorating ideas for minimum fuss so it's easy for my mom to clean.

A. Think about the kitchen first. Have doors put on all the cupboards so there are no open shelves where things gather dirt and grease. Don't litter the counter tops with small appliances that will also need cleaning. Tuck them away in the lower cupboards so they're handy but out of the way.

For the rest of this large apartment, get Mom a vacuum cleaner with attachments for cleaning both the rugs and bare floors. Don't use mini blinds as part of your window treatments. They require a lot of dusting.

Put collections of small items in a curio cabinet and avoid knick-knacks that clutter up surfaces — a real pain to clean around. Better to accessorise your home with art work and other types of wall hangings.

And here is some unsolicited practical advice: pick up after yourself and keep your bedroom tidy. Hire a part-time maid to come in a couple of times a week to give the kitchen and the bathrooms a good scrubbing, wash the windows and help out with the laundry. If that's not in the budget, pitch in and do your share to lend Mom a hand.

Q. We're moving house and wonder if we should just start over.

A. Don't think you must throw out everything and start over when you move house albeit the new one is a different style of architecture with different colour schemes. Starting over from scratch is an expensive, and often unnecessary, proposition.

Take most of your things with you, then ponder the situation. Upholstered furniture that looks wrong in its new setting can be recovered or slip-covered and even restyled. Wood pieces can be refinished or painted. Even old drapes

Neutral Zone
This neutral colour scheme that is right for a quiet, relaxing mood is found in Robert Mathis's living room.
Photo by Pallon Daruwala

can be reused by taking them apart and making swags, valances, cafe curtains, pull-up blinds — the possibilities are endless (*see Chapter 8*). If you end up with extra furniture that cannot be used anywhere, you can always get rid of it later.

CHOOSING COLOURS

Q. How does one decide on a colour scheme?

A. What are your favourite colours? Have a look inside your wardrobe to check out the colours you wear most often. This may give you some ideas about which colours you are comfortable with. If you go for strong or unusual shades, remember that you may eventually tire of them. A house that is full of bright colours can become nerve-wracking.

Another approach is to select a colour scheme that creates a certain mood or one that is closely tied to a theme you like. As you build your files, this will become clearer. Keep looking and snipping.

Q. What colours go together? I can't make any sense out of colour charts.

A. You can study colour charts and colour wheels until you're blue in the face and still not understand colour. There's a more practical way to learn about the subject. Go to fabric stores and study bolts of material. Look at floral, striped, plaid, and figured fabrics. When you find something you like, ask for a sample. If you choose a stripe or a pattern, be sure the sample is big enough to show the entire colour

spectrum. Add these to another folder marked Colour Schemes. Later you can decide where you're going to use what and place it in the appropriate "room" folder.

Start paying more attention to nature's colour palette. Take snapshots of gardens and flower arrangements that you like. As you browse through magazines, watch for pictures of these things. Tear them out and file them in your Colour Schemes folder along with your snapshots.

Q. We want our new dream home to be a peaceful haven with lots of open spaces. What colours should I choose?

A. Colour schemes have a lot to do with environmental mood-setting. If you are especially sensitive to colours, pick your colour scheme first, then select a theme that is in keeping with the choice. To establish a restful feeling, try new shades of pastels like the softest-to-die-for colour combinations of turquoises or greens and pinks.

For another up-to-the-minute look, choose the easy-going neutrals that build around shades of black, white, grey, beige, and taupe which can be mixed and matched. Or, focus on one neutral such as off-white and mix it with several other variations from cream, bisque and bone to ivory. Neutrals go with almost any style including formal, casual, country, traditional, and *avant-garde*[1].

Q. When going for a new colour scheme, where do I start?

A. The starting point is the most important thing in the room. For example, in the bedroom the bed will be the basis from which you work. Start by selecting a new bedcover and sheets. The colour, pattern and style you choose will set the mood. Paint the walls to blend with the new bed set. Curtains

---

1. *Avant-garde:* cutting edge, unorthodox, daring, or innovative styling.

will also be coordinated.[1] Change the wall hangings to suit the mood. Congratulations — you have a new bedroom.

Tip: Safe isn't always right. Stark white walls and beige marble flooring are not right. Walls should be in a tone that correlates with the floor. Dark Oriental furniture looks better and is more harmonious with coloured walls. Use colour to pull things together, especially when you're working with different elements in the same room. For example, if you have a contemporary dining set against a Chinese wall screen, pick a colour from the screen for the dominant tone. Pick it in varying shades and contrasting colours on the walls, rugs, drapes, and on the upholstery for the chairs.

CREATING THE MOOD

Q. How do I know what looks and themes will suit my personality and our lifestyle?

A. Write down this list of adjectives: conservative, flamboyant, ordinary, dull, playful and amusing, strong and bold, graceful and elegant, offbeat, whimsical, relaxed, quiet, dramatic, sophisticated. Now check off those words which describe your personality.

Then write down these words: formal, informal, simple, traditional, casual, modern, sophisticated, unconventional. Go over this list, and check off those words which describe your lifestyle.

Remember those files that you are so diligently compiling? As you periodically edit them, look at these two lists. Do the pictures you have saved relate to your personality and lifestyle?

Pull out those that do not apply. Your surroundings should reflect your inner self so that you will be comfortable and happy. You should not make your home into something you're not. For example, if you have an offbeat and whimsical personality with an unconventional lifestyle, you aren't going to be happy in a sophisticated, formal environment. Never mind the pretty pictures.

Now we'll explore various decorating themes, and you decide what sounds like the real you.

Country Look: there are many kinds of country mainly because the word is so overused. Basically, the feeling is warm and cosy and the mood is informal and relaxed. Furniture can be wood, wicker, upholstered, or overstuffed as used in English country styling. Wood pieces are usually simple, supposedly to reflect simple country life. Fabrics are normally printed or checkered but can be solid colours as well. Fabric choices are usually linens, cottons and chintzes. Colours are strong — red and blue with grass green or bright yellow; fresh pinks and greens.

Rustic: while some people include rustic in the country category, I prefer to treat it separately because it doesn't give me that same warm and fuzzy feeling. However, you can call it whatever you want to. The furniture style is simple and unpretentious, sometimes even crude. People who like textures and shapes often go for this look because surfaces are coarse and rough. Walls are textured plaster or done in brick, stone or wood. Floors are also a natural material like wood, stone or brick and scattered with thick, heavily textured rugs. The whole idea is back to nature with the basics.

---

1. You can use matching or coordinated sheets for curtain fabric and as slip covers for bedroom chairs.

Contemporary: means different things to different people, but all agree that this is a clean, safe look that's never really in and never really out. In the strictest terminology, furniture is functional, high-grained and polished. Walls are usually painted white or beige. Fabrics are simple and practical. Art work is serene and serious and framed in fine wood. There's no room for frills or whimsy in a truly contemporary setting.

However, to many people, contemporary means today's style which is best described as uncluttered eclectic — a mix of the old and the new. Each piece of furniture has it's own space and purpose. Stress is placed on objects being the best one can afford. Neither of these contemporary looks is cheap to accomplish.

Modern: this look is more dramatic and elegant than contemporary and somewhat more flexible. Furniture is classic and simple in design often combining glass, chrome and leather. Fabrics are sleek and neutral. Walls are often white. Floors are usually wood, tile or marble covered with Oriental rugs or elegant free-form area rugs. Accessories are sparse.

A more formal version of the modern look might have upholstered furniture covered in white silk with splashes of colour in satin throw pillows. Serious abstract paintings are in order.

Hi-tech: this is an open, almost office-like look. Its trademark is simplicity in design and materials. The hi-tech room should be exclusively hi-tech — no mixing is allowed. Lines, being the key word, are square or rectangular, no curves. (Are any of you Agatha Christie fans? Doesn't this describe Hercule Poirot perfectly? For example, he says the world will be a perfect place when chickens lay square eggs.) Furniture is low and compact. A modular sofa upholstered in

grey with a coffee table of thick glass floating on a black lacquered triangle typifies the look. Walls are flat and smooth, painted with ordinary paint or high gloss enamel. Flooring is plain square tiles set in narrow grout. Black or chrome track lighting is used. Windows are covered with metal blinds, vertical or horizontal. Accessories are red, black, white, and grey with lots of black rubber. Art work is bright, bold and modern. If you're an efficiency expert, you'll love calling a place like this *home.*

Period or Traditional: refers to any style that's not current and can cover any past period, including everything from neoclassic, Mughal and Colonial to art deco, art nouveau, and the popular Retro craze. Since hardly anybody can afford to do up an authentic period room, original items and antiques are commonly mixed with reproductions and modern look-alikes. The furniture is more finely crafted than country, smoother and more highly polished. Fabrics are more elegant. Walls can be painted or wallpapered in traditional patterns. Ceilings often have crown mouldings or lacking that, are faked with wallpaper, handpainted or stencilled borders. (It's the effect that is important — not necessarily the real thing.) Preferably, floors are highly polished wood and covered with Oriental rugs.

This look is for those of you who treasure your heritage and find comfort in history. It's always in style and is never a passing trend. If you tend to resist change, you will be comfortable in this setting.

Regional or Tribal: based on a cultural look like Rajasthani, Balinese, Tibetan, and Mexican.

Eclectic: a complex mixture of several different styles that should be tied together for a total look,

Setting the Stage
The mood-setting
entrance hall in
Melinda Alexander's
bungalow is
furnished and
accented with her
predominantly
Chinese collection.
Photo by
Peter Mealin ≥

which is usually done with colour and feeling. It is not a hodgepodge. It takes experience and taste to successfully put together an eclectic setting. Somehow it defies description, but it works nonetheless.

Q. What goes into getting the country look? I'm dying to give my flat a laidback cosy feeling and think this is the way to go.

A. Of the many variations of country, three styles are especially good here. English country works for apartments where cooped-up indoor living is the norm. The idea is to make the place feel cheerful and cosy. To create this look, go for upholstered and slip-covered furniture done in a mixture of colours and patterns. Floral chintzes are preferred. Be generous with room accessories to clutter up things. Work with irregular groupings and odd numbers like using three candlesticks on the table instead of a pair. Put hand-crafted items and vases of flowers around, stack books and magazines in baskets, and scatter rugs on the floors to complete the look.

If your flat has a balcony and you prefer a more indoor-outdoor lifestyle, Mediterranean country is a better choice. It's a colourful, minimal look that's suitable for small spaces and open-air living. The colour scheme should be cool greens, Mediterranean blues, sunny yellows and oranges. Simple curtains and painted furniture, textured walls and painted floor boards make for a well-used, comfortable setting.

The third kind of country that is often used in India and southeast Asia is British colonial. It's a simple, nostalgic look characterised by white walls, cane and folding/portable furniture, coir rugs, mosquito netting, wicker baskets, white lace, and books. Windows are often left bare except for louvered shutters that protect against the weather and provide privacy. Otherwise, they are covered with white, filmy fabric or lace.

Q. How can we get a country cottage look without getting too rugged? We love natural things but aren't into rustic. Is it something that gets boring after a while?

A. Because the cottage look originated in the countryside, it is based on decorating with simple, natural things. These days you can bring the look downtown by using lots of floral, striped and gingham fabrics to imitate a natural setting. Leave off the rough-looking ceiling beams and stone flooring to stay away from a rugged feeling.

To keep from getting bored with the look, don't get too fussy or contrived. Anything that's too cutesy doesn't wear well.

Q. I love antique furniture that is heavily carved in the traditional style. But the pieces are too big for our flat. What do you suggest?

A. Complete sets of traditionally-styled furniture are hard to cope with. Today's smaller homes and apartments cannot accommodate them, and dark, heavily carved and inlaid with mother-of-pearl sets do not blend with modern decor. However, there are ways to incorporate traditional pieces with today's lifestyle and have the best of two worlds.

Instead of using whole sets, decorate with a few traditional antique pieces or reproductions, mixed with other furniture. Many items can be altered to suit today's lifestyles. For example, since antique mahjong tables are only about one metre by one metre, the legs can be cut off to make coffee tables. There is a wide variety of items that offer many other possibilities: cabinets of all sizes (a large one can be used as a TV and/or stereo cabinet, small ones used as end tables and bedside tables), chests, chairs, display cases, and stands (used for plants and *objets d'art*).

The old colours of blackwood and rosewood do not

mix well with modern looks. So, refinish pieces in lighter shades. The natural colour of both woods is much lighter than one would think and is lovely when left in its original state and sealed with a clear finish.

Here's another idea for using the old look in a new setting. You can have custom-made rosewood and teak reproductions done to any desired size, style and colour to work in perfectly, providing that at least a picture with dimensions and a colour sample is supplied for copying. Be sure that the wood has been sufficiently dried and that floating panels[1] are used to prevent cracking and warping (ask the furniture crafter for a guarantee).

Tip: Every so often wood furniture can be polished with beeswax. For daily cleaning, wipe with a damp cloth only.

Q. I've noticed that many antiques are made out of blackwood and rosewood. What are the differences between them? Is one any better than the other?

A. Blackwood is so called because in olden times it was painted black. Actually, its natural colour is very close to rosewood, but the grain is closer together and nicer than rosewood. In addition, it is heavier than rosewood. Old furniture with mother-of-pearl inlays normally is blackwood. (In modern times mother-of-pearl is also used in rosewood.) Now blackwood is very expensive and becoming rare. Blackwood is often preferred over rosewood because of its higher value.

Rosewood is the least expensive of the hard woods, has a reddish colour and is virtually knot-free. Antique pieces were not highly lacquered, but new pieces are. When left in its natural state or sanded down, the wood has a lovely grain that usually cannot be seen through the dark stains. Many different styles, including European designs, are available even in antique pieces.

Both blackwood and rosewood are used for carving because the harder wood lends itself to delicate carving. Time and artistic talents for carving are better spent on hard wood which is inherently more valuable than soft woods.

Tip: Don't pass over the softwoods. Many old pieces, especially chests, were made of softwoods such as elm, camphor and boxwood. Even well-crafted new pieces are worth collecting for their future value. Elm is attractive and the most popular. It is a light coloured wood usually styled without a lot of detailed carvings. Lacquered pieces with hand-painted designs like old Chinese chests were usually made from soft woods. Designs were painted on after lacquering. New and old, they make lovely accent pieces.

Q. When we purchased an antique chest, the shop owner volunteered to clean up the brass fittings. The result is disastrous! Some of the brass is shiny while the rest is still in its original condition. How can we make the fittings look uniformly old again?

A. Perhaps the brass can be oxidised to restore the old look. Take the piece to a well-known, respected antique dealer for advice. They will know what to do. Best not to try a home remedy because you might make a bigger mess.

---

1. Floating panels: panels are not permanently affixed to allow for expansion and contraction of the wood due to changes in temperature and climate.

Tip: Brass on old pieces should be left in "as is" condition.☙

Q. I would like to have a rich traditional Indian heritage look for my new home. Could you please help me in getting the right colour scheme for my house? My favourite colours are purple and blue.

A. A strong traditional theme will give your home drama and individuality. Use your favourite colours, purple and blue, in rich intense shades with metallic gold, bright green and magenta[1]. Go all the way to complete the look — make lamp shades out of filmy sari fabric and use antique Indian furniture for accent pieces.

Q. I think the simplicity of pinewood furniture is great, but my fiancé claims it will make our home look dull and lifeless. How could I liven up the place?

A. Go eclectic by combining the naturalness of pine furniture with splashes of bold colours, lively patterns and daring accessories to create your own plucky sense of style. Use geometric tribal rugs or durries under the dining table and scattered around the living room and bedroom. Go for zany tableware, modern window treatments and show-stopping bed linen.

Mix things up with wicker, natural or painted, in accent pieces like a living room chair, bedside tables or a small storage chest to prevent the monotonous look of too much matching furniture. Top off the look with some whimsical lamps and accessories.

Q. Please help us decorate our flat. My husband and I are professional people with a very hectic lifestyle, and we hate housework. We spend every holiday sailing and love anything nautical. We can't stand fussy prints, clutter or antiques.

A. Use your passion for sailing as a guideline to planning and decorating your home. For a nautical colour scheme, go with blue and white in stripes, plaids and checks with splashes of sunshine yellow.

Unadorned mini blinds in bright blue are suitable, easy-care window treatments. Canvas Roman blinds in solid blue or wide blue and white strips are another option.

The simple lines of Scandinavian styled furniture, either painted or in a natural finish, would fit in with the theme. Canvas deck chairs are comfortable for watching TV and lounging, and directors' chairs are great at an informal dining table.

Accent the decor with shell and starfish collections, an aquarium of tropical fish. Add potted palms and capiz[2] lamp shades. Decorate with fabrics in white, muted pastels and beiges.

To keep housework to a minimum, make sure you have plenty of built-in storage space for stowing away everything from kitchen appliances to books and magazines — anything that collects dust. Keep table tops free of knick-knacks. Instead, accent your rooms with wall hangings — a few nice paintings, prints or framed theme posters.

Q. I'm a real nature lover who is stuck in a concrete and glass apartment building. Besides the obvious, lots of plants, what can I do?

---

1. Magenta: a vibrant shade of pink with blue tones.

2. Capiz: a translucent shell material used to make decorative objects.

A. Use the setting to your advantage and create the feeling that makes you the most comfortable. Simulate a lush tropical garden with arrangements of fresh and artificial flowers such as birds of paradise, bougainvillaea and, of course, orchids of all sizes and colours. Suspend a *papier mâché* parrot among tall green plants. Pick up the theme in curtains, throw pillows and upholstery. Accent with green and white stripes or get wild with animal prints like faux leopard, zebra, etc.

Or, transport yourself to an English garden. Arrange dried or artificial hydrangeas and roses in wreathes and porcelain bowls. Hang baskets of geraniums and ivy. Use floral chintzes lavishly.

ARRANGING THE FURNITURE

The way you arrange your furniture and accessories will have a profound effect on the over-all look and feel of a room. You can have the most gorgeous stuff in the world, and no one will be able to appreciate it if the room doesn't make sense. To do that, you must first think about what will happen in this room. Is it a living room where you will entertain friends and relatives or a living room where your family will relax and watch TV or read or work on hobbies? Or is it all of those things. Let's say it's the latter — sort of a multi-purpose room. You will want a conversation area that can handle extra seating — I suggest floor pillows that are easily stashed under the coffee table or in a corner when not needed. Put the TV on rollers so you can roll it out of the way or into another room temporarily.

You need to work with empty space when arranging furniture. So, move everything out. Pick a focal point. It can be a window with a view, an architectural feature of the room like a niche that holds an interesting sculpture, or a painting. Whatever it is, that's what you will make the centre of attention. Bring in the largest or most important piece of furniture. After you have placed that piece, bring in the second largest piece, and so on. You must never lose sight of your focal point as you place the furniture. When you are satisfied, start adding in the side tables, lamps and other accessories.

Be aware of traffic patterns — in other words, how people will move around the room. You must leave enough space for walking so people won't bump into things. If you have to go through one room to get to another, arrange the furniture so that no one has to walk through a conversation area or in front of someone who's watching TV. Small irritations like that can make you feel really cramped up.

BUDGETING YOUR MONEY

I have a lot to say on this subject. We all work with some kind of budget. The rules for planning and spending this budget are the same whether you have a fat wallet or a skinny one. Again, it's my turn to ask the questions. As you fill in the answers, the picture will become clear.

How much can you realistically afford to spend on the entire project? How much can you spend immediately? How much will you have a year from now or five years from now to continue the project?

What things do you need to budget for?

Does the place need any structural repairs or modifications?

In what condition are the plumbing and electrical systems? Do they need repair and/or updating to meet current standards?

What about the kitchen and bathroom(s)? Do you need to spend any money on these rooms? In what condition is the tiling? Do the floors need repairs or replacing? Do you need appliances like a cooker and a refrigerator?

What pieces of furniture do you absolutely need: beds, dining table and chairs, living room sofa?

Do you need lighting fixtures and/or ceiling fans?

For sure the place will need painting. You will want some pieces of furniture in addition to those you need. And, you will have to cover the windows with something. You will also need accessories like rugs, lamps, sheets and towels, and wall hangings such as pictures and mirrors.❧

Getting Prices

So far, you have just been doing your homework and making lists. For the next phase of decorating, you will need lots of patience and some comfortable walking shoes. It's time to find out how much all this is going to cost.

For all projects, including structural work, repairs, painting, furniture making, and window treatments, you will need to get at least three written estimates. Be sure the estimates include cost of materials and labour. Other important pointers:

Personally check out the quality of the contractors' work by thoroughly inspecting projects they have completed.

Do not pay anybody in full until the project is completed to your satisfaction.

All contracts and agreements including date of completion should be in writing.

Once a contract is signed for a certain amount, the price cannot be raised later on. For example, the persons involved cannot say, "Oh, so sorry. But the price of paint, drapery fabric (or whatever) has just gone up, and I'm going to have to charge you more." If someone tries such tactics, you must say, "I'm sorry too, but that's your problem." Any substitutions must

be of the same quality for the same price as stated in your written agreement.

Here's another common pitfall: the painter says, "I'll charge you for two coats of paint on each wall." Wrong! It's a common practice to water down the paint to make it go farther. So, here's what happens: you've paid for 45 litres of paint, but he only uses 27 litres. He pockets the extra money, and your walls look awful. What's the right way to avoid this happening? Write in the contract that the paint job must meet your approval.

Source and price out all items like appliances, furniture, light fixtures, bedding, lamps, absolutely everything you have on your list. Do lots of comparative shopping.❧

Adding It Up

After everything is itemised at the very best price available, total it up. I guarantee you're in for a shock because it doesn't matter how much you thought it was going to be, it's going to be more. And unless you are very, very rich, it's going to be more than the amount you have on hand for immediate expenditures.

What then? Well, first of all, don't give up the project out of despair. Study your list long and hard, and ask yourself the following questions:

What can I do without for now? A few easy things to eliminate right off the bat are expensive side tables and a coffee table for the living room, and bedside tables. You can make a table out of just about anything like a ceramic garden stool with a piece of glass on top (*refer to illustrations in Chapter 2*). Or get some cheap used tables and cover them with a cloth that enhances your colour scheme.

Where can I compromise? For example, instead of replacing those kitchen cabinets right away, perhaps a couple of coats of fresh paint will do the trick for now. Instead of buying a new sofa, maybe you can slip-cover an old one.

Can I do up one or two rooms now and the rest later? Of course you can. Just remember to keep your grand plan in mind so you won't end up with a hodgepodge.

How much of the work can I do myself? Probably a lot more than you ever thought. "Necessity is the mother of invention." And in these days of higher prices and bigger expectations, we are learning to do things for ourselves. Anybody can learn to paint, and most everybody can learn to sew a straight seam.

But, don't be "penny wise and pound foolish." For instance, it may be cheaper in the long run to have the whole place painted at once instead of having the painter do up one room at a time. Ask him. Be aware of which items may go up in price in the future — like appliances. And don't skimp on quality. If your choice is between one expensive chair that you love and two or three cheaper ones that are just so-so, buy the one which you love and use floor pillows for now. Don't skimp on upholstery fabric for a sofa that's going to get a lot of wear and tear. But it's okay to go for a mid-price fabric for a chair that isn't used much — like maybe a bedroom chair. Also, don't skimp on bedding. Good mattresses last longer than cheap ones that wear out quickly and are uncomfortable besides. One last word about bedding — buy the biggest size you're ever going to want. Another example: my newly-married friend was buying their first bed set. My advice to her was the same, "Buy queen or king-sized, dear."

She said, "Oh, no! The sheets and bed covers are so expensive." So, okay, she bought a double-sized mattress set. Two years later, she upgraded to a queen and it cost her a bomb.

Q. How can we decorate our new home without making expensive mistakes?

A. There will be mistakes — even the pros make them — but with careful planning and attention to details, you can keep them to a minimum. Go slowly. Do comparison shopping by getting two or three price quotes. Buy the best quality and workmanship you can afford. And most important, never assume anything.

It must be a hands-on experience that requires working closely with the contractor and making lots of decisions personally about things you never thought about before like where the light switches should be and which way do you want the doors to open, in or out?

Work with reliable people. The best way to find them is through friends' recommendations. Then be sure to get everything down in writing, including small details. Plan to spend a lot of time on site checking out the progress. Remember that it costs less to correct mistakes as you go.

Q. Our house looks like an architect's nightmare! The exterior is a mish-mash of different elements because it's old and has been subjected to several unique trends over the years. We've just bought it and, after decorating the interior, there isn't anything left in the budget to redo the outside. How can we improve on the outside without spending a fortune?

A. At the risk of sounding like a broken record, I have to say it once again — paint is the cheapest and fastest way to cover up uglies. Here are some tricks for outside painting.

Take an objective look at the good and bad features of your house. Hide unsightly gutters, downspouts, metal awnings, pipes, and other such appendages by painting them the same colour as the house. Use neutral hues for big expanses of wood trim and shutters, and go all out to highlight small, interesting details like mouldings and architectural accents with a contrasting colour.

It's fashionable now to use colour more bravely, but the over-all scheme must be tastefully done. Decorators advise choosing muddy shades rather than clear tones that look garish in bright sunlight.

Q. We will be moving into our new apartment soon and would appreciate your advice on purchasing furnishings and decorations. Basically we are a working couple with a young, five-year-old son and enjoy entertaining friends.

A. Go for an uncluttered, easy-to-maintain look that suits your busy lifestyle, with a warm and inviting feeling to make your guests feel comfortable. Let the general architectural design of the apartment be your guide for style. Stick with a basic colour scheme throughout if most of your rooms are directly or indirectly accessed from a combination living/ dining room. Use the same tones in various combinations and shades, with different accents, to give each room its own personality. Read decorating magazines and books for colour and style trends that will work for you, then canvas furniture stores and decorating shops for availability and prices. Talk to their in-house decorators for more ideas. Go slow! You don't have to decide everything at once.

Tip: Don't decorate your home in a mode that is not suitable for your family. Elegant, but delicate upholstery fabrics, hand-rubbed table finishes, antiques and fragile accent pieces may not withstand the everyday use and abuse of little children. You will end up spending an inordinate amount of time warning the children to be careful and worrying over your investments. Consider your family's ages, personalities and current needs, as well as their whims, then make your choices accordingly. When there are young children about, use more durable furnishings in public areas and their bedrooms. Keep delicate elegance in your bedroom which should get less wear-and-tear than the rest of the house.

Q. My fiancé and I will be moving into a temporary place when we get married until our new flat is ready. Now our big headache is choosing furniture that will be suitable for both places.

A. There's a very simple guideline to remember when buying furniture — good taste and quality never go out of style. Be prepared to spend a wad of cash, though, because quality doesn't come cheap. But here's some advice.

Don't buy on impulse. Shop around and look at every thing. When you find something you really love, go back for visits to see if you keep loving it.

Stay away from trendy, gaudy, cutesy, and different to the point of being weird. Keep it simple at the beginning. The minimal look will be great for you because it's easy and practical. Anyway, your first apartment will probably be on the small side so less is better.

Go for traditionally styled basics, i.e., dining table, sofa and lounge chairs, and set your theme with accessories like lamps and accent pieces that don't cost the earth to replace when you move.

Tip: Don't buy trendy furniture when you have a limited budget. You will find that it goes out of fashion rather quickly, and you are then stuck with things that have become dated. Remember water beds? Study furniture trends before investing your hard-earned money. Go to the library and read back issues of major decorating magazines published 10 to 15 years ago. Out of every mod period, a few good things become conventional. You will soon discover what has survived the test of time and, therefore, will always be in vogue. Decorating tip: Use trendy accent pieces, accessories, and window treatments to achieve a with-it look.

Q. Our home is starting to get that tacky unloved look. What can I do to make it look better without spending a lot of money?

A. Why not give your home a redo? Don't say you can't afford it. Of course you can. Here are some easy ways to spiff up the place and do some simple decorating at the same time, without breaking the bank.

For starters, **get rid of all the junk** you've let accumulate — and be tough about it. The rule is: if you haven't used it or worn it in the last year, you don't need it and won't miss it.

Next on the agenda is **reorganising storage space** like kitchen cupboards, wardrobes and closets. Take everything out, sorting as you go, and wash the shelves. When it's all sparkling clean, put away those things you just can't part with.

Make the most of available cupboard space; buy some plastic or wire stackable trays. Get some racks to hang on the inside of cabinet doors — great for getting those messy spice jars organised and for storing dishwashing odds and ends under the kitchen sink.

Take down the curtains and drapes for washing or sending out to the drycleaners. A word of caution: know what kind of fabric you are working with. Before you throw anything into the wash tub, make sure that both the curtain and lining are washable. When in doubt, send them off for drycleaning — which also can be a risky business if you aren't sure the drycleaner is reliable. Ask around for recommendations from people who have had good luck. Then cross your fingers and hope for the best.

Clean the wood furniture with a cloth that's wrung out until it's barely damp. Then wipe off and buff with a soft dry towel. Refurbish the wood by rubbing it down with Melamine Oil, available at hardware stores. Let the oil soak in for several hours, then wipe thoroughly.

Shampoo the rugs. Take them outside and beat them to death before the rug cleaner comes. Getting out the loose dirt makes shampooing easier and the end results are better. Check out the yellow pages of the phone book under Carpet Cleaners for listings when you don't have a direct referral. Choose a company that guarantees their work. And, have them clean the upholstered furniture while they're at it. Don't forget to ask about prices. Get everything in writing, please.

Then **give the floors a good scrubbing**, especially in the kitchen and bathrooms. Go to the super market and read the labels on the backs of floor-cleaning products. Choose one that fits your kind of flooring; i.e., if the floors are wood, pick something recommended for wood. Be careful to choose a non-abrasive product for surfaces that scratch easily like marble, ceramic tile and terrazzo.

Wash off the walls. Remove all fingerprints and smudges, especially around doors and light switches. Use a mild dishwashing liquid detergent and a clean, preferably new, sponge. Do not use old dirty rags which compound the problem and smear the smudges around.

Replace those worn-out lamp shades. If you like the size and shape of the old one, take it down to a lamp shop and ask them to copy it. On the other hand, if you hate it or want a whole new look, take the lamp with you and try on different sizes and shapes to see what works.

Now, stand back and have a look at everything. If the place still looks dingy, you probably need to **give the walls a fresh coat of paint.** There's nothing like it for a quick fix. When you can't stretch the budget to hire painters, make it a weekend project for the family. Or call in friends and make a party out of it. Bribe them with lots of food and drink.

Rearrange the furniture. The difference will amaze you. Rooms take on a whole new look, and it's fun to play around. For an afternoon's entertainment, invite a friend over to help you shove furniture. (Moving furniture works better with friends than with husbands.)

Decorate the walls with pictures. They don't have to be masterpieces of art to be effective and give you pleasure. Framed prints, photos, and even attractive calendar pictures can make good wall decorations. (***For more on this subject see Chapter 10.***)

Set out fresh flowers and potted plants for instant decorations that give a homey, lived-in look. Flowers can be all one colour, or shades of the same colour, to match with the room's accents, or mixed in colour and variety to pick up all the different colours in the room. The choices are many, but whatever combination you use, flowers should look like they belong in that particular room and in that particular spot.

Potted green plants are good anywhere. Real is best but, when you can't be bothered, artificial is okay. Use them in corners to fill up empty spots, next to lamp tables to cover up electrical cords or on the kitchen window sill just to cheer you up. If you go for the real thing, be sure the plant suits its environment. For example, cacti don't do their best in humid spots like bathrooms, but money plants can make it almost anywhere.

Now you have some practical pointers for giving your home a quick fix. You will be drop-dead surprised at how fresh and new the place looks and feels when the project is completed. Everyone will admire your cleverness and wonder how you managed a redo. Don't tell them. Just smile and change the subject.

CREATING MORE SPACE

Creating more space is a national pastime for all of us. We are obsessed with the idea that we have to make rooms seem bigger because somewhere we heard that bigger is better. Well, it would be nice if all our rooms were large, but most of us aren't so lucky and there's not much we can do about it. The challenge is in doing the best we can with what we have and making it work for us. You should never look at a room and say, "Ugh! This room is too tiny and too awful, and I can't do anything with it." You must always have the upper hand over your environment. You should approach problem rooms with the idea that, "I can make this room look better and put it to better use." Attitude has a lot to do with success.

Q. What are the rules for decorating a small room?

A. There are a few important things to keep in mind. The size of the furniture used in small rooms should be in proportion to the size of the room. You don't want to make the room look like a dollhouse, but you should probably think like that to keep yourself on the right track. In other words, don't put an 2.5 metre (8-foot) sofa in a small living room. Go for a smaller version, maybe even a two seater. The same rule applies to the chairs. Don't pick big, over-stuffed armchairs. You need less bulky furniture like streamlined chairs with wooden or metal arms. Consider selecting a glass-topped coffee table because it appears to take up less space. To give a small room an organised look, balance the furniture arrangement.

Upholstery, drapery and bedcover fabric patterns should also be in proportion. Large, splashy prints will be overwhelming and, therefore, are probably out. The same is true of busy prints because they make a small room look confusing. Instead, go for uncomplicated, coordinated prints that have a regular pattern like stripes and plaids. Patterns in muted shades are very good, too, or decide on a monochromatic[1] colour scheme to make a small room seem

---

1. Monochromatic: all one colour or different tints of one colour.

larger. (For an excellent example of a balanced, mono-chromatic room, refer to the *photograph* of Robert Mathis's living room on *page 14* of this chapter.)

Another rule of thumb is to keep the window treatment simple. Don't go for an elaborate, multilayered look in small rooms. I don't like voluminous balloon shades either. It's too much. Go for a flatter, less full look like Roman shades. But that's another subject that you can read lots about in *Chapter 8*.

One last word about small rooms: never underestimate the value of mirrors for expanding space. For example, my friend who had a small apartment in Tokyo didn't like the closed in feeling of the dining area. So she mirrored the wall opposite the balcony, which brought in light and doubled the view of the outside greenery. The result was a sense of openness that automatically made the room seem bigger.

Q. We're wondering how to use the open area under the staircase of our flat. Or, since space is so important, should we put in a spiral staircase instead?

A. Check the regulations of your apartment building before you start ripping out the staircase. A spiral staircase may not be an option. Are there children or elderly relatives living in the house? If so, please be aware that spiral staircases aren't the safest thing around. They can also deter potential buyers should you ever want to sell your flat.

I recommend utilising that space under the stairs and making it a focal point. You have a number of options.

Turn it into a quiet reading area. A comfortable chair, foot-stool and floor lamp is all you need.

How about a study corner for the kids, or a place to pay bills and write letters for yourself? Add a small desk with a clip-on halogen lamp, and a chair, foot-stool. *Voilá!* You're in business.

Here's another idea: a custom-built mini bar with cabinets or open shelving above for glasses, a washable counter-top for mixing drinks, and closed cabinets below for the liquor.

Q. Our small flat is very short on storage space. How can I improve on something I don't have?

A. There's probably more room available to you than you know. The idea is to utilise every square inch of space. In the following chapters, you will find room-by-room storage tips, but here are a few general pointers that apply to the whole house.

The main thing is to buy furniture that does double duty. Look at every piece as a potential storage space: a trunk that serves as a coffee table or topped with cushions, becomes extra seating.

Side tables and bedside tables should have storage space below — shelves and/or drawers. Get a storage unit to house the TV and stereo equipment that has space for tapes and CDs. (Preferably one with doors that you can close when the TV is not in use.) Use the top to display books or collectibles.

Don't waste that extra foot or so of space above wardrobes and kitchen cabinets that builders love to leave empty. Close in the space between the top of the units and the ceiling with either matching, custom-made cabinets or shelving. There's an added bonus to this: it provides some protection against noise.

Walls aren't just for hanging pictures — you can use them to hold shelving so you don't take up floor space with free-standing cabinets and book cases. Put shelves in every possible place, even the most unlikely places like over the toilet, windows and doors. Just be sure they are well anchored so they don't fall off and hit you on the head.

If you have a bathtub, get wire racks that hang from the

side to hold toiletries. If you have a shower, install racks to hold things. Baskets are nice for towels, but if you don't have floor space for them, be sure you have enough towel rods, pegs or hooks.

Don't overlook that valuable space under your bed. If you can't have a bed with built-in drawers underneath, get some inexpensive flat boxes that you can stash under the bed for storing linen, blankets and even extra clothes.

Welcome to the World of Home Decorating
A young Hindu woman creates a Rangoli
outside the front door to welcome all who enter.
The traditional design is created from
tinted crushed powder and is considered an art form.
Photo by Pallon Daruwala

CHAPTER 2

Living Rooms

INTRODUCTION

Houses have always had a central gathering place, or living room, of some sort. In the past, this room was known by any number of aliases like the lounge, the hall and the drawing room, to name a few. Whatever it was called, it was a special room, frequently only used on holidays and other important occasions as a place to entertain friends and relatives. It was usually off limits to the children because they might (heaven forbid!) touch the lovely, breakable things set out for display.

Then, along came television, which changed our lives and revolutionized the way living rooms were used. People had to find a place for the new contraption — a room that was big enough for everybody to gather around the tube. The logical place was the living room, of course. And gather they did.

Since television sets were few and far between at the beginning, "Come over to watch TV tonight" became a social rallying cry. I firmly believe that the popularity of television was the single biggest influence on the way living rooms were, and in many cases still are, decorated.

Not only were rooms rearranged so that all the furniture faced the TV set, more comfortable and durable furniture that could stand up to daily use came on the scene. Snacks and drinks were served to the viewers in the living room and, of course, the children were included. Therefore, the upholstery and floor coverings were changed to stand up to spills and messes. Informality ruled as the stilted, conventional-looking drawing rooms of the past became history.

The lasting result of this giant shift in lifestyles is the way we utilise the living room. Now we know that this room need not be held in awe. We can actually use this room for what its name implies, *living*.

STEPS FOR DECORATING

The first step in decorating the living room, as with any room, is to decide how it will be used. The size of your home will be the determining factor. If the living room is the only gathering place, it will be a multi-purpose room where you entertain and where the family collects to play games, read and watch the inevitable TV set. Or, it may be used as a living and dining room combination.

Next, you must look at the architectural features, if there are any, and the proportions of the room. Is the room long and narrow with low ceilings? Is it square and boxy with high ceilings? Does it have awkwardly placed pillars or columns?

After carefully considering what you have to work with, you can choose the type of decor, style of furniture, floor covering, and colour scheme that will best suit your lifestyle. Yes, you will face complications along the way, but the following real-life problems and solutions will help you overcome these dilemmas.❧

Q. We are a newly married couple in our first flat and have acquired an interesting collection of furniture from well-meaning relatives. Some of the pieces are beautiful, but we don't know where to put them or how they can be used.

A. Bless those well-meaning relatives because they've done you a great service! Not only have they given you some much-needed items, it is because of their generosity that you will learn a valuable decorating lesson: rooms that are creatively put together with pieces that have a history are much more interesting than instant, store-bought decor.

Anita Nair and her husband have collected some lovely old furniture and have used it in very innovative ways (**photo opposite**). For example, the antique shaving stand that belonged to Anita's grandmother is used in the dining area of their flat as a cupboard to hold table linen. An old stand of open shelves, which one would normally expect to see along a wall, is in the middle of the room and serves as a divider to visually separate the dining and living spaces.

The old hatrack that's flanked on both sides by bentwood-styled chairs makes a good ballast for the shaving stand and gives the right perspective to the furniture on the long wall. They have found that it's a wonderfully handy item to have near the front door. Anita pointed out that although some of the furniture is tall, many pieces, including the dining table and stools, are unusually low. She feels that since the flat is small, the low pieces allow for more space around them, which is effective in creating the feeling of bigger rooms. The low, rope-sprung chairs in the living room are among Anita's favourite pieces — they were purchased with her first pay cheque.

Q. We have a long living and dining hall combination. How do I break up the space into two areas without renovating or using something obstructive like a screen? We want to keep the open feeling.

A. You can visually break the room into two distinctly separate areas simply by grouping the furniture according to its use. The *illustration on page 34* shows an arrangement that was planned out for Kavita Gopalan's flat.

Furniture is pulled away from the walls to create a loose, floating arrangement. Both areas are clearly defined by conveniently locating the dining table next to the kitchen and grouping the living room furniture to make a cosy seating area at the other end. The conversation zone is pulled together with an area rug[1].

---

1. Area rug: so called when a rug is used to define a given area.

Mixed Blessings
Anita Nair and her husband have acquired several antique pieces, including an old shaving stand from her grandmother,
which is now used to hold table linen in the dining area. Photo by Pallon Daruwala

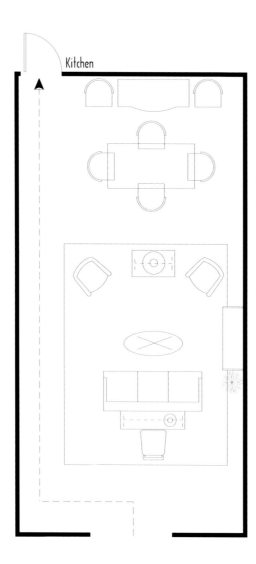

Kitchen

For this arrangement, you will notice that the sofa works best with its back facing the front door. To get a more finished look, a narrow table is placed behind the sofa. By adding a lamp and a chair, the sofa table is turned into a convenient writing desk.

The furniture placement allows for good traffic flow from the main entrance to the kitchen so groceries can easily be hauled through without cutting across the conversation area.

Q. Our living room is unusually narrow (3.5 x 9 metres/ 11 x 30 feet) with windows across one end. What can we do to make the room seem wider?

A. Break up the string-bean look by placing the furniture in an L- or U-shaped arrangement. If you're using a three-seater sofa, coffee table and side tables, don't put them on a long wall. Lining up furniture makes things worse. You need to create cosy conversation areas so you don't have to shout from one end of the room to the other.

Don't turn on a bright ceiling light that evenly illuminates everything at once. You will want to go for lamps and area-lighting techniques to pull the eye to furniture groupings or interesting objects rather than instantly focusing on the entire room.

Hang mirrors opposite each other on the long walls close to the end with the windows. This is a visual trick that pushes out the side walls and widens the room.

Put down rugs with a horizontal geometric pattern, and use a horizontal window treatment.

Q. I want a very formal look for our living room, but it's small. Is it okay to go formal in a small room?

A. Yes, you can go formal in a small room. Why not treat your living room as though it were an old-fashioned parlour? If heavily carved Victorian furniture isn't to your taste, give it today's look of simple elegance. For a beautiful example of formal, unfussy decorating, study the ***illustration opposite*** which features the stylish parlour in the home of Carol Ratcliff. This room wins the prize for simple elegance.

Since this is a room for adults, Carol felt comfortable selecting an all-white, monochromatic look for the sofa and chairs with throw pillows covered in old sari fabric for a dash of spice. Although solid colours are great for the look, a small discreet pattern or subtle two-tone stripes are good too.

Carol selected a brass and glass coffee table that plays up the brass handles on the antique chest, the gilded mirror and the brass lamp. To anchor the coffee table, she used

Old-Fashioned Elegance
Formal sitting rooms like Carol Ratcliff's are back in vogue. These rooms are purposely rather small to allow for intimate, grown-up conversations. The decor and feeling should be appropriately adult. Rendering by Sheryl Perry ❧

S. PERRY '97

an Aubusson[1]-inspired rug, which also pulls together her colour scheme.

Architecturally, this room is blessed with a high ceiling and tall windows that are covered with sheer panels and silk swags. But you can get the same formal effect if you don't have tall windows and high ceilings. You can fake it by raising the curtain rods and using deep valances[2] to hide the wall between the ceiling and the window. I've often used this trick to create the illusion of tall windows, which also makes the ceiling look higher.

Q. My sofa is covered in a floral pattern with a midnight-blue background and touches of bright yellow. Can I paint the living room bright yellow? What about extending the same colour throughout the apartment, including the kitchen?

A. I have recently seen this colour scheme used in the living room, and it was smashing! However, I urge caution when using such a vibrant colour all over the house because there are some disadvantages. For instance, bright yellow looks very warm, like strong sunshine, and can be overwhelming in a small place. Also, yellows tend to darken with age. This is especially a problem in kitchens when the paint is exposed to grease and grime. All things considered, it's not the best choice for most Indian kitchens.

Therefore, although you most certainly can go for bright yellow in the living room, I recommend using lighter shades of yellow like rich cream in the other rooms and off-white walls with bright yellow trim in the kitchen. You will get the same effect and a softer, cooler feeling.

Q. We're having a problem choosing our living room set. The walls and floor are white, and the doors and wood trimming have a brown finish. I love the look of white and wood, but we want a cosy feeling.

A. The effect of all white and wood is terrific and can go in several directions, including cosy. Here's how: choose an over-stuffed living room set, slip-covered in a heavy, textured cotton or a white-on-white Kashmiri crewel[3] fabric that's cleanable. I advise selecting a slightly off-white colour because pure white won't stay that way for very long. In fact, it is wise to have at least two sets made at the same time so you can switch them out when it's time to clean them.

For added cosiness, toss a paisley shawl over the back of the sofa or armchair. Don't arrange it too carefully — make it look as though you've just taken it off and temporarily laid it down.

Bring more wood into the room in the coffee table, side tables, and accessory pieces. Remember that the woods don't have to match, but you should use some pieces that are similar to the doors and trimmings to tie things together.

Cover table tops with Battenberg lace[4] — a square napkin placed in the centre of a small round table or a square napkin

---

1. Aubusson: originally copies of Turkish designs woven in Aubusson, France. Eventually associated with a more European than Middle Eastern look, frequently having a floral motif.

2. Valance: a soft fabric skirting hung at the top of a curtain or drape.

3. Kashmiri crewel: a type of embroidery commonly used on hand-woven drapery and upholstery fabric. Technique brought to Kashmir by Middle Eastern traders.

4. Battenberg lace: a type of lace originating in Europe and made popular by Queen Victoria around the turn of the last century, and so named when her daughter married into the Battenberg family of Germany. (The Battenbergs of England changed their name to Mountbatten during WWI.) It is now readily available and affordable.

laid diagonally on a square table. That way, only part of the table top is covered, which allows more of the wood to show.

Q. I'm going for an informal, homey theme. What about a living-room furniture set in light peach or light yellow leather, or should I settle for something in brown to match the wooden side tables and coffee table?

A. Cool, pastel-coloured furniture like peach and light yellow won't give you the look you're going for. Think about warmer colours, but not brown. All-brown furniture is boring and would kill your wood tables.

I would turn to earth tones for warmth. For example, furniture in dark green or dark blue leather, terracotta lamps, kilims[1] or tribal rugs, and throw pillows covered in bright patchwork, appliqué, or blockprinted designs are effective elements for a homey look.

Another of my favourite comfortable colour themes is a burgundy leather sofa; arm chairs upholstered in navy blue, hunter green and old gold striped fabric; brass lamps and a Persian-design Indian rug in predominantly dark blues and deep reds.

Tip: Leather furniture lasts a long time, so you have to think hard about your colour choice. Stay away from mod, trendy and bright colours because you may tire of them long before your furniture wears out.

Q. The architecture of our flat has a contemporary feeling. Also, the walls and floors are stark white, which emphasize the hard lines and unusually high ceilings of the rooms. Do we have to go with modern furniture? We really hate it.

A. Usually decorators say interior decor should follow the architecture of the building — some are quite firm in this opinion and others are more flexible. Because we can't always find a home that completely fits our criteria, I agree with the latter group as long as the project is well done. Life is made up of little compromises, and this is one of them.

However, I do believe the best way to handle situations like this is to go for an unobtrusive decor — something mildly eclectic. Strong traditional themes that include cushions on the floor and low tables will be inharmonious with tall, cathedral ceilings[2].

The ***photo on page 38*** is an excellent example of what I mean by a mildly eclectic setting. In her living room, Joan Griffes has effectively mixed Chinese and Indian accessories and rugs with conventional upholstered furniture. It's her clever use of colours and fabrics that makes these different objects come together. The colour scheme of brown and blue is derived from the upholstery on the sofas.

The terracotta brown that's so subtle in the sofa fabric becomes a dominant colour when the rugs and pottery are added to the room. And the soft blue that's barely noticeable in the sofa fabric becomes the other major colour for her decorating scheme. There's nothing glaring about Joan's white walls and floors because they are now merely the background for her furniture and accessories. In the end, she has also successfully downplayed the high, sharp pitches of the living room ceiling by pulling the eye down and into the graceful dignity of the setting.

Q. How can we blend an elegant purple leather sofa set and

---

1. Kilims/Kelims/Khilims: flat-woven rugs that may have originated in Kashan, Iran.

2. Cathedral ceilings: very tall, pitched ceilings patterned after those found in many churches.

a black-glass hi-fi cabinet with tribal pieces for a cosy, uncluttered atmosphere in our living room?

A. Tie the various elements together and create the mood with fabrics. Tribal material often has touches of delicious purple tones mixed in with other interesting hues that can be picked up for accent colours.

Use the fabric for drapes, throw pillows and table scarves. Scatter some kilim rugs around on the floor and make a wall hanging out of an antique textile to complete the look.

Q. I'm afraid that a three-seater sofa is too big for my small living room. What are my options?

A. Go for a two-seater sofa (love seat), one or two armchairs — depending upon available space — and an ottoman, all of which should be in proportion to the small sofa. An ottoman is especially handy because you can prop your feet on it or use it for extra seating. You can also put a tray on it and use in place of a coffee table. Put the ottoman on casters so you can roll it around to wherever you need it.

Q. Is cane[1] suitable for a living room set?

A. Of course, but you must provide the proper atmosphere for it. Cane belongs in a casual setting. Cushion covers should also be informal and made of cotton, linen, canvas, or raw

◀ *Mildly Eclectic*
The living room in Joan Griffes's home is a quiet mixture of treasurers gathered from around Asia, including Indian terracotta pottery. Photo by Pallon Daruwala ❧

silk. Heavy brocades and velvet fabrics are too dressy for cane.

Cane works best when it's mixed with other furniture like old wooden pieces or antique colonial, which don't have to be the real things — but do go for the best reproductions you can afford. An old dowry box makes a great coffee table, and planters' chairs also work well with cane.

Another way to liven up cane furniture is to mix it with novelty items. The ***photo on page 40*** shows how Maureen Berlin used a stack of handpainted tin boxes to add interest to a pair of Victorian-styled cane chairs. The boxes became a table for a large terracotta lamp. Notice how the colours on the boxes are repeated in the durrie rug.

I've used all cane furniture (sofas, chairs, coffee tables, and side tables) for informal settings in two different homes and grew tired of it in both places, too much of the same thing. But Maureen's perfectly coordinated setting has colour and variety, a combination that would never be boring.

Q. I want cane furniture in a natural finish for the living room, but the walls are almost the same colour as the cane. Should I paint the walls a different colour?

A. Not necessarily. To paint the walls or not depends upon your over-all colour scheme and the look you want to achieve. The natural colours you're talking about provide a soft, neutral background for any way you go. The style of the cane furniture you select will determine what kind of theme the room should have. These days, cane is available in everything from Victorian to *avant-garde*.

The next step is to have cushion covers made for the cane in colours and fabrics suitable for your theme. Then,

---

1. Cane: hollow, jointed bamboo stems. Differs slightly from rattan, which is solid stems of slender palms. Both materials are used for wicker items.

Easy-going Comfort
Cane furniture can work in just about any casual setting when lively and interesting accessories are added. Photo by Pallon Daruwala

go for rugs and window treatments that coordinate with the cushions. See *Chapter 10* for more about colour schemes.

Q. Little piles of red dust have appeared under our three-month-old cane chair. Although we were assured the chair had been treated, I strongly suspect it is now bug-infested. To complicate matters, the cane shop has gone out of business, so I cannot go back to complain. Is there something we can do before the whole chair disintegrates?

A. The chair probably was initially treated. However, the poison that is commonly used kills only the bugs, not the eggs. In the period of time you have had the chair, these eggs have hatched. There is a simple treatment you can apply yourself. Put kerosine in tin cans and set the chair legs in the cans. The raw cane on the inside of the legs will absorb the kerosine and kill the bugs, which are most likely wood borers. I was told kerosine will not damage the finish — I hope they are right. If the style of the chair does not lend itself to this method, examine the cane carefully, looking for tiny holes. Use a hypodermic needle to inject kerosine into the holes. You may have to repeat the treatment in a few months because these new bugs probably have been busy laying eggs too. At any rate, you must either treat the problem or throw out the chair because the bugs will eventually march over to the next piece of furniture and take up residence.

Q. I have a three-seater rattan sofa in the living room and also plan to buy an antique rosewood sofa. Can you mix up different styles of furniture in the same room?

A. You can make it work if you have a large room and arrange the pieces in two separate groupings. In a small space the styles are too different to be compatible.

Pull the room together by using the same fabric for the cushions and tossing around mix-and-match throw pillows on both pieces. Be sure to stain the rattan sofa in a rosewood colour to match the antique sofa.

Q. How can I breathe some life into our living room? It feels like a furniture showroom that could belong to anybody.

A. You need to add some personal touches. Here's how: first, strip down the room to its bare essentials, removing everything like lamps and accessories from all the surfaces. If you have any pictures or mirrors on the walls, take them down as well.

The next step is to make sense out of your furniture arrangement. Do you want it grouped together for chatting with your friends or a bit more casually laid out for sprawling around and watching TV? This is the first phase of personalising a room because you're shaping it to suit yourself.

Bring the lamps back in and put them around where you need them. Check the lamp shades for dirt and grime — they may need replacing. You may want to bring in a lamp that you've had in another room. Or you may want to add a new one. Even lamps can be personal. I have a bronze elephant that I made into a lamp. I looked a long time for just the right elephant, and when I found him, I was thrilled. I have the lamp on my desk now, and it makes me smile to look at my magnificent find. Search your home for things you want to have around you.

Put out lots of fresh flowers in your favourite containers, which don't have to be proper vases. An old copper pitcher, an unusual tea pot, or an oversized drinking glass will do — as well as just about anything else that takes your fancy.

Make a grouping for the coffee table, using items in different sizes and shapes. Add a couple of your favourite books to the table for balance.

Study the **photo opposite** to see how Maureen Berlin put personality plus in the living room of her flat by grouping collectibles in a casual display.

Q. The light-coloured wood finish on our beautiful living room set is an eyesore! It's yellowish and spotty looking. Is there a home remedy?

Also, I'm changing the colour scheme in the living room to peach, white and ivory. Will this suit the furniture? What kind of upholstery fabric do you recommend?

A. Forget about a DIY[1] job on that finish. The upholstery will have to come off so the old wood finish can be stripped and redone. A real professional should have no problem fixing it up for you.

Your new colour scheme will complement the light-coloured wood, but do go for an upholstery fabric with a classic design, not geometrics, to get a dressed-up look.

If you have a collection that's appropriate for the living room like brass candleholders, betel-nut cutters or handworked silver boxes, put it on display. What could be more personal than a private collection (**photo opposite**)?

Finally, re-hang the pictures and mirrors. You might want to move them around a bit or change them —

◄ **Candles Galore**
Maureen Berlin's main sitting area is a perfect example of a highly personalized room. Maureen's collection of candlestands and other accessories from India and southeast Asia are used to add the finishing touches.
Photo by Pallon Daruwala ❧

sometimes that's all you need to make things look and feel right.

Tip: Keep in mind that lampshades don't have to be white, nor do they all have to match. The proportion, colour, shape, design, and material of the shade should go with the lamp. There's no such thing as one size fits all when it comes to lampshades.❧

Q. After removing a wall to make the living room bigger, we're stuck with two awkward pillars. How can I hide them? Should we raise the floor to make them shorter and less noticeable?

A. Pillars are hard to camouflage — even short ones, so forget about trying to hide them. Instead, use a clever furniture arrangement to diminish their importance by drawing the eye away from them. For example, in front of one pillar place a free-standing panelled screen that suits your decor to serve as a background for a table and chair grouping. People will notice the setting and not even see the pillar.

If one of the pillars is wide enough, treat it like extra wall space. Put a rectangular table against it with a vase of pretty flowers, and hang a picture on the pillar. This allows you to use the table and pillar as an end piece for an L- or U-shaped sofa arrangement.

Q. The pillars in the living and dining area of our flat stick out and cause the room to look smaller. How can I make this area seem less crowded?

A. As much as we'd like them to just disappear, ugly

---

1. DIY: means do it yourself.

pillars are often awkward things we just have to live with. But you can make them less offensive by working the pillars into the overall decor. Treat them like room dividers to define the different spaces and to separate the living and dining areas.

At the risk of repeating myself, I have to pass on this advice one more time. To visually create space which will make the room seem bigger and the furniture less crammed together, mirror the pillars.

Q. What can I do with a small alcove off our living room? We can use the extra space, but we don't want to spend a lot of money to do it up.

A. Space is in short supply these days, so every little bit counts. Grab the chance to create a cosy little multi-purpose corner. A rather awkward space at Geetha Chetty's home was turned into an attractive conversation area-cum-TV room. It also doubles (or triples) as a guest bedroom. Here's how to get the look: purchase a low, futon-styled sofa[1] that folds out for extra sleeping space. Be sure to measure the alcove before you go shopping. You need enough room to unfold the sofa cushions. Use big, floor pillows like these for extra seating. They are easy to stack in a corner at bedtime too. Small places and simple accessories seem to go together. Interesting artwork spot-lit with track lighting is all the decoration that's needed here. Clean-looking Roman blinds on the windows and a bi-fold door, attached to an overhead track, provide privacy for overnight guests. On ordinary days you and your family can use this area for reading, playing games, chatting with friends, and watching TV.

Tip: If futon-styled sofas are too expensive or unavailable in your area, you can easily have one stitched. All you need are three thick, foam-rubber cushions cut to the size you want. Cover them with a durable fabric like heavy Indian cotton or canvas, leaving enough fabric between each cushion for folding. Run seams along the end of each cushion to hold it in place. When it's folded up, two cushions form the sofa seat, and the third one forms the back. Since the bottom of this third piece rests on the floor, it must be tall enough to fit behind the other two folded cushions with enough left over for leaning against.

Q. We like the idea of a spacious, minimal look for the combination living and dining room, but the dining table seems to clutter up things. Any ideas?

A. You need a different kind of table. Drop-leaf tables and console-type tables that pull out are styled to do double duty. To keep the living room lean and clean, work one into a grouping as an accent piece and use it as is for an intimate dining spot. For parties and festivals open it up and spread out the food.

You might want to choose a game table with comfortable-looking club chairs, upholstered to fit in with your living room furniture. Go for a table with an extension leaf to accommodate more people on those special occasions.

---

1. Futon-styled sofa: a futon is a Japanese cotton-batting mattress, used either directly on the floor or on a low frame. However, futon-styled furniture has become a generic term for soft items, placed on the floor, which unfold to make a bed or fold up to form a chair or a sofa.

ARRANGEMENTS AND TRAFFIC FLOW

Q. We have no walls in the living room. It's all open space with a glass sliding door to the balcony. What can we do with the TV and sofa?

A. Here's your chance to get up-to-date in a more relaxed setting. The modern way is to move furniture away from walls and form groupings for easy conversation. Your sofa can go in front of the sliding door, leaving room for access to the balcony. Armchairs go in the open space across from the sofa. Put the TV on a swivel-top table or on wheels so you can roll it around to get the best view.

Q. I am so upset over my husband's newest acquisition. He bought a big-screen, hi-tech multi-system TV and parked it in the living room. I realise there is no other place to put it, but the soft, cosy look of the room is totally ruined. What can I do?

A. It's unfortunate that electronics displayed in a living room that is not designed specifically for the enjoyment of hi-tech equipment can spoil a carefully planned motif. However, most men don't seem to notice.

My advice is to hide the entire system in a cabinet or armoire that coordinates with your look. There are lots of beautiful old wooden *almirahs*[1], and painted Kashmiri and Rajasthani pieces around that can be converted to suit your system. But if you can't find anything to your liking in the shops, have a furniture maker design a cabinet or wall unit with doors. Before you begin the search, do your homework. Think about the size, placement and number of components that must be housed. Measure everything and take the dimensions with you when you go shopping.

Q. Visitors have a clear view from the living room straight into the bathroom. How can I solve this problem?

A. You can screen off private spaces by placing a room divider in front of the door to create a small entrance way. If the door opens out, be sure to leave enough space so the bath-room door can swing open and shut in an unobstructed way.

You can go for something permanent and have a divider built in. Glass blocks are wonderful because they don't appear to take up space, and they allow light to shine through. Or choose a hinged screen for a divider that you can move around. Place a potted plant next to it. If there's room, incorporate a chair and a side table to make a furniture grouping.

Portable dividers come readymade and made-to-order in a wide range of styles, including painted, etched and stained glass; cane; wrought iron; and cloth. You can also go for old wood doors hinged together. Select something that works with your living room decor.

Q. How can I arrange the furniture in my tiny living room to make it look bigger? I have two armchairs, a two-seater sofa, a rectangular coffee table, a round dining table with four chairs, and a long cabinet which holds the TV and stereo.

There are sliding glass doors at the end of the room which lead to the covered balcony.

---

1. *Almirah*: a large Indian wardrobe.

A. Sunita Banerjee's situation was very similar to the one you described. Here's the solution which worked for them, and I think it will do for you as well.

The glass sliding doors made it easy to visually extend the room by incorporating the balcony into the living and dining space. All of the furniture was arranged into groupings, while treating the two spaces as one room. In doing this, the glass doors were totally ignored to create an open concept.

Obviously, the dining table and chairs were placed at the end of the room near the kitchen. The sofa and chairs were arranged in a U-shaped grouping as illustrated. The entertainment centre went against the wall opposite the sofa. You will need to add a small, round table with a lamp at the end of the sofa next to the balcony.

The glass sliding doors were left free of any kind of window treatment because drapes would divide the space rather than extend it. If privacy or strong sunlight is a problem for you, mount either *chiks*[1] or canvas roller blinds on the end of the balcony cover so that they will drop down behind the railing. This also allows you to use the balcony space even during the rainy season. In fact, I favour using *chiks* over canvas blinds because they permit some flow of air and still offer protection against the rain.

The balcony was turned into a furnished, mini garden with lots of green plants. For interest, a small fishpond was added, which may or may not be possible in your case — if not, put an intriguing rock formation in place of the pond. The narrow hedge that runs along the railing is not only pretty to look at, it's a safety factor as well to prevent children from climbing around on the railing.

The patio table provides a place for alfresco dining and also increases the dining space so more people can be accommodated. I added ceiling fans to make the balcony

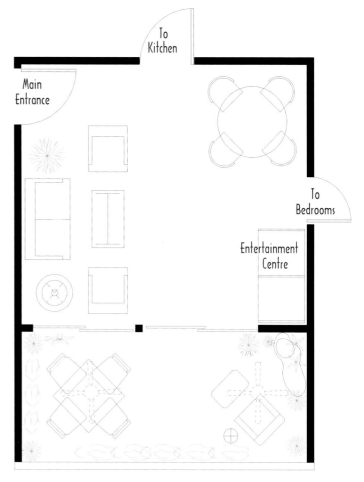

The Banerjees' living/dining room "grew" when the covered balcony was incorporated.

more comfortable during the hot season and to help drive away the mosquitoes.

Q. We've been advised to knock out the common wall between the living room and the guest bedroom to make the living room bigger. I hate to lose an extra room though. Any ideas?

A. Replace the existing wall with some handsome bi-fold doors that could be opened up whenever you want. Furnish

1. *Chik*s: bamboo chick blinds.

the old bedroom space with a sofa bed or, for a more current look, a day bed, and create a seating area for watching TV. The folding doors will be a handy feature to provide private space for guests and to close off a blaring TV when the rest of the family want to chat or just read in peace and quiet.

Tip: Before knocking down any walls, be sure that you aren't about to destroy one that is load-bearing.❧

Q. The previous owner of our home removed several walls to create an open concept, but I don't know what to do with all this space. Should I reconstruct some of the walls?
We need a dining area, a TV area, a reading corner, and a place for the desk and our computer. I don't know how to divide the areas.

A. My advice is to try several different furniture arrangements to see how they work for you and your family before you start putting up walls again.

Arrange your furniture into groupings according to the activities which will be performed in that area. Place the dining area close to the kitchen for the sake of convenience. Now, look around at the room. The TV area will probably take up the most space, so you should work on that next. Since the sofa is usually the largest piece, place that first and go from there.

To keep the room from looking chopped up, I would combine the work area for the desk and your computer with the reading corner. Use the space that's farthest from the TV for maximum privacy. Place the desk and computer first, then add in a comfortable chair and a good reading lamp. I suggest a floor lamp on one side of the chair or a standing halogen lamp with an adjustable arm behind the chair. On the other side of the chair, put a small table to hold a tea cup or a beer glass, and you're all set.

Q. I hate the traffic pattern through our living room (below), but I can't come up with any other way to place the furniture. Please help!

A. Not only is your traffic pattern bad, you've got a lot of wasted space in the middle of your room. In addition, your sofa, chairs and bench are so far apart your guests must have to shout at each other to be heard. Ideally, for comfortable conversation, the furniture

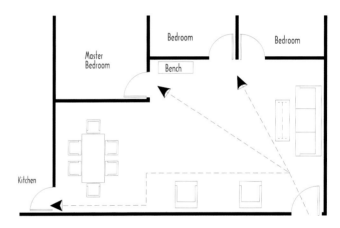

Before: poorly arranged furniture makes for an awkward traffic pattern. ❧

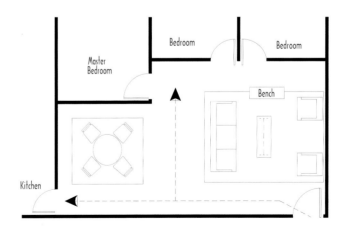

After: the new arrangement makes more sense and allows traffic to flow smoothly through the room. ❧

should be no further than 2.5 metres (8 ft.) apart.

Don't worry, though. Your problem is an easy and inexpensive one to correct. Once again, the solution is to rearrange your furniture (*below, on page 47*). Form a conversation centre by shifting around the sofa and chairs and pulling the bench into the grouping.

The other change I recommend is to sell that over-sized dining room table because it blocks the entrance to the kitchen. Purchase a round table with an extension leaf to use when you need a bigger table. I chose a round table instead of a square one because you already have so many corners in the living room. However, I've unified the room by using two square area rugs.

Look how the new arrangement has created lovely, un-obstructed walkways to the rest of your home. Amazing, isn't it?

Q. We've lived abroad, and I picked up some Chinese antiques. I've also managed to find several pieces in India as well. Will you please give me some ideas for using these pieces in our house?

A. For this, I refer to the home of Melinda Alexander, who brilliantly decorated her old bungalow with odds and ends from many parts of the Orient (*photo opposite*).

While the locally-made upholstered furniture is simple, the room is charged with dramatic colours and textures, which are inherent in Oriental pieces. Her accessories are Chinese and Indian with a few European accents. Melinda is never timid about mixing up things.

The sheen of the silk sari fabric casually thrown over the chair adds depth as it pulls the eye across the room. It ties in beautifully with the old rugs and the Chinese chest. If you don't have quite as many Chinese treasures as my friend does, I suggest you enrich your collection with more Indian accessories. For example, marble-topped

rosewood south Indian or Goan tables can replace the carved Chinese tables, and a painted Kashmiri chest can be a substitute for Melinda's Chinese chest.

Q. How many tables do I need in the living room, and where should they be placed?

A. There is no formula to dictate the number of tables you should have in a living room. For that matter, they don't all have to be, literally, tables. What you do need is a surface of some sort that is located within reach and is approximately the same height as the arm of the sofa or chair it's next to.

Think about what the surface will be used for. If you're going to put a lamp on it, you can use a small chest that's just the right height. If you want something to set coffee cups or drink glasses on, you can convert unusual items into tables (*photos on page 50*). Wooden and ceramic elephants, sturdy baskets, large ceramic planters, and terracotta pots all look great and are very serviceable with glass tops added. Very substantial bases can hold marble or granite tops if you prefer.

Tables all over the room are rather boring, and decorators unanimously agree that something different is more interesting. Also, small chests used as side tables can store some handy items such as games, coasters, napkins, and extra candles. You can take this idea a step farther by making a coffee table out of things like a pair of ceramic elephants with a glass top cut to any size you need. Or, go for a camphor chest with an interesting fabric thrown over it to protect the surface.

As for placement, the coffee table should be 30 to 50cms (12 to 18 ins.) from the sofa to allow space for knees. Tables and other surfaces should be, as I said, within reach. Try it out—sit down with a glass in your hand, and then reach out to set it on a nearby surface. If you feel comfortable, it's in

Oriental Splendour
Melinda Alexander's accessories are Chinese and Indian with some framed European prints and a large tapestry
thrown in for good measure. Photo by Peter Mealin ❧

Something Different
Top left: **Depending on the size of the terracotta pot and marble top, this combination makes a side table, a coffee table and even a dining table.** ❧

Top right: **Together, these mismatched ceramic elephants make a coffee table. Separated with smaller glass tops, each works as a side table.** ❧

Middle left: **A brass plant stand topped with a round serving tray can go in a formal setting.** ❧

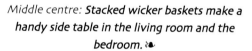

Middle centre: **Stacked wicker baskets make a handy side table in the living room and the bedroom.** ❧

Middle right: **An old sewing machine base topped by granite, marble or glass is a real conversation piece.** ❧

Bottom left: **This wicker elephant makes a novel side table for an informal living room and a good bedside table, especially in a child's bedroom.** ❧

Bottom right: **The terracotta horse planter topped with a piece of round glass makes a great side table and works with a variety of furniture styles.**
Photos by Pallon Daruwala ❧

the right place.

Tip: Glass-topped wood furniture needs small pieces of felt placed between the glass and the wood so the glass won't stick to the furniture during damp weather.

Q. Should I have a coffee table as well as tables at both ends of the sofa?

A. A coffee table in addition to side tables for the sofa is not an absolute requirement. However, I have found that when we entertain, I always end up placing a small table of some sort in front of the sofa for that middle person, during those times when I'm not using a coffee table. Therefore, if space or the budget is a problem and I had to make a choice, I'd go for the coffee table — or a reasonable facsimile. (**Refer to the previous Q&A for optional ideas for a standard coffee table.**) A surface in front of the sofa is more convenient for guests than tables at each end of the sofa.

Q. The top of our coffee table is completely ruined from setting wet glasses and coffee cups on it. What to do?

A. Here's a quick-fix idea I picked up from a lady, who said her aunt solved a similar dilemma by spreading old sari pieces over the table and then covering the whole thing with a glass top.

I think this is a gorgeous idea whether your table is in bad or good condition. It's a wonderful way to add colour and interest to your room. The old sari pieces would make a lovely background for displaying collectibles too.

Q. How can I conceal the drain pipe from an air-conditioner that runs the length of the living room wall next to the ceiling? Major renovations to move them are out of the question.

A. Box up the pipe with plywood and paint it to match the walls. The whole thing will blend together beautifully, and you'll hardly notice it. In fact, if the budget permits, you can use this as an opportunity to enhance the lighting in the living room. Install some canister or halogen spots in the bottom of the plywood box, and add a dimmer switch for mood lighting.

CHAPTER 3

Dining Areas

INTRODUCTION

Whether you dine in a lavishly decorated, formal dining room or in a casual eating space in the kitchen, your surrounds are important. This is the place where everyone gathers at least once a day to catch up on each other's activities, to gossip and most importantly, to stay in touch with one another. For the sake of your family, your friends and yourself, you should create a warm and friendly atmosphere that encourages communication.

While many of us still long for a proper dining room, just as many will not see this wish fulfilled. Because dining is much more casual now, dining areas are taking their place. Another reason they are disappearing is simply practicality. The dining room is a very expensive area. Most families have alternate, informal eating spaces, either at a table or a snack counter in the kitchen or on a balcony or a patio or on a tray in front of the TV (which I don't encourage). In these instances, the dining room becomes the least used room in the house. When you figure out the price of the space per square foot and the expense of the furniture, lighting, floor covering, and decor, it's a very costly room! Many people these days decide against having one. If they are building, they very often go for dining/living room combos, or designate a spot in the living room for a multipurpose table, so they can spend that money elsewhere in the house.

Regardless of where the dining spot ends up, a separate formal room or a designated area, the setting should be decorated to enhance the pleasures of eating, whether you are in the company of others or alone — in fact, I'd say especially if you're alone.

FORMAL

These days formal dining doesn't follow the stiff modes of conduct dictated in the Victorian era, which does not mean that good table manners are out of fashion. *Au contraire*, good manners ensure pleasurable dining. It does mean that a more relaxed form of conversing takes place in a formal setting — a separate dining room isn't even necessary. A well-decorated eating space and a beautifully dressed table, appropriately set with your best crockery and glassware, are the only essentials in creating the right environment for formal dining.

Q. How can we give our dining area an elegant formal feeling without buying heavy and stodgy furniture that costs a bomb?

A. Formal entertaining doesn't mean you need an elaborate dining room set. Go for the unexpected to make things more interesting (*photo opposite*). A room can have a strong, elegant feeling using simple, mismatched elements. Here's how you can do it on a shoestring budget.

Cover a nondescript table with a beautiful cloth and napkins.

Get chairs with simple lines that fit into most settings. Although they don't have to match, the seats should be the same height and the backs work best

◄ **Visual Delight**
Simran Gupta designed an eye-catching table for intimate dining in her Bangalore flat. Her innovative approach to decorating literally explodes with colour and textures for a sensually dramatic effect. Photo by Pallon Daruwala

when they are at least similar in size.

Use a sideboard for extra serving space. You can make one out of anything. For example, an old, painted chest works to add a splash of colour.

Set the table properly with your best crockery and glass-ware. Usually, formal tables are set with matching plates, glassware and cutlery; but I've seen mismatched items used, including cutlery, for a most elegant effect.

Add candles and flowers.

Wear a smile and treat your family and friends as honoured guests — that is the cheapest element of all that makes for a truly elegant feeling.

Q. Is it possible to get a formal look with a regional theme, or is it meant to be casual?

A. Atmosphere is the key element for creating a mood, so to make a regional theme feel formal, dress it up. See Melinda Alexander's Chinese-style dining room on *page 56* for a fine example of out-of-the-ordinary formal.

Q. I'd like more flexibility in decorating our dining room. Once long ago, a friend had a chair rail[1] in the dining room. She used novel combinations of paint and wallpaper in a variety of ways to achieve totally different settings. Are chair rails still in style?

A. Chair rails are as strong as ever. Quick and easy to install, they provide a multitude of ways to create different moods whenever you want something new. Choose a wood moulding in proportion to the room size and ceiling

---

1. Chair rail: a strip of molding placed on the wall to protect the wall from chair scrapes and bangs.

Dressed-up Dining

An unlikely portrait of George Washington watches over Melinda Alexander's gloriously appointed, formal Chinese-style dining room. The picture is a favourite of Melinda's husband and hangs in all their homes. Photo by Peter Mealin

height — narrow for small rooms and low ceilings, wider for large rooms and tall ceilings. The placement height also greatly depends upon the ceiling height — about 76 cms (30 ins.) for normal ceilings and more for taller ceilings. To judge what is right for you, have someone hold a piece of the moulding up to the wall; then stand back and look at it. You'll know when it's positioned correctly. After the chair rail is installed and before painting, be sure the nail holes have been filled with wood-filler compound and sanded for a smooth finish.

Paint the new chair rail and woodwork to contrast or coordinate with the walls. Or paint the chair rail and below a shade darker than the wall above the rail. Or wallpaper above the rail and paint below — or vice versa.

Although chair railing originated in eating areas, they don't have to stay there now and have become a handy decorating tool. Expand the treatment to other rooms and dreary corridors. Paint the rail to your liking, then use a wallpaper border just above it. Patterns set the mood. Parade ducks, bunnies or stars around a child's room. Select a lacy or floral border for the master bedroom. The possibilities are endless.

Q. The dining room in our otherwise spacious apartment is rather disappointing. Although long enough to accommodate the furniture, it is disproportionately narrow and gives one a crowded feeling. Is there a solution to this problem?

A. Short of moving a wall, which is usually not practical, there is nothing you can do structurally. But do not despair — the room can be visually widened to alleviate the claustrophobic feeling by using mirrors on one of the long walls. If cost is no object and the landlord doesn't mind, mirror the entire wall or a large portion of it. A cheaper alternative is a very large, framed rectangular mirror

hung horizontally. Either way, the room appears to double in width.

P.S. Make the table centrepiece and opposite wall attractive because you will be seeing double.

Q. I love the grandeur of a long dining table with tall chairs, but somehow we ended up with a round table and very low-backed chairs. How can I decorate my dining room to inject an air of elegance?

A. Round tables do have a comfortable, friendly feeling, but you can also get a very classy look. Create a formal background for dressy table settings to get the mood you're after.

The previously discussed chair rail idea works wonders in situations like this. Paint the part below the railing a solid drama colour — red, dark green or a rich blue. Above the rail do one of the new wall treatments like sponging, ragging or faux finishing. If there is a moulding at the top of the wall or the ceiling, paint it a slightly lighter shade than the chair rail. If not, top everything off with a wall paper border.

You will also need a smashing chandelier on a dimmer switch for soft subtle lighting.

Use tablecloths and napkins in damask or solid colours. Place mats are too casual — sorry about that. Also, you should use silver flatware with your best china and crystal. Don't forget the candles.

Q. I can't stand knick-knacks, but I like traditional furniture, which usually calls for lots of accessorising. Is it possible to keep our dining room simple without all the frills?

A. Yes. These days almost anything is possible if it's done with taste and feeling. You can see how Robert Mathis gives

new meaning to the word "traditional" (*photo opposite*). While the architectural features of his dining room give it a traditional ambience, the sophisticated elements he added (and those he omitted) keep it lean and sleek. Spicy-cinnabar walls, modern art and wrought-iron chairs are right at home with a hand-carved antique table, marble columns and classic black and white marble flooring. The result is the ultimate in modern traditionalism — without accessories and knick-knacks to clutter the look.

INFORMAL

Q. The fabric on the seats of our dining room chairs is soiled from spills made when our children were small. I need to redo them, but I'd like a good idea for something out of the ordinary. Our lifestyle is relaxed and informal.

A. Tribal fabrics with handstitched designs and Kashmiri crewel make wonderful chair-seat covers. They are especially interesting when different patterns are used. There are no particular rules to follow except that the colour spectrum should be similar because fabrics in soft shades don't mix well with vibrant shades.

Q. Ours is a small, three-room flat. How can I arrange the furniture in my tiny living/dining room to make it look bigger? Where should I place the table? There is a row of windows at the end of the living room, which overlook a

◄ Warm and Spicy
Strong colours are all the rage, and Robert Mathis's spicy-cinnabar dining room makes a dramatic statement. The warm hue compliments the richness of his antique table and chairs. The look is on the formal side, but the feeling is friendly and inviting. Photo by Pallon Daruwala

miniature balcony, but it's too small to use for outside dining.

A. You can visually expand a small space by tricking the eye with interesting focal points and mirrors. Turn the balcony into a mini garden with lots of green plants and some attractive garden accessories like a stone frog and toadstool or small terracotta animals. The eye travels farther to have a look at things outside and makes the room seem bigger.

As for furniture placement, don't chop up a small room by trying to create separate dining and living room groupings. Just think of the space as one area that incorporates the dining table.

After that, there aren't any rules. Move things around until you find a combination that feels right. Try angling armchairs and pulling furniture away from the walls when it makes sense.

To make the room look twice as big, use a large framed mirror as a wall decoration, choose a three-panelled mirrored screen for a corner, or go whole hog and mirror an entire wall.

Q. I have a small dining/living room combination. Should I partition these two areas in some way? The pine dining furniture matches the living room sofa set.

A. A structural partition between the two spaces will make them looked crowded. With your matching sets, a visual break is all you need. Use a tall, strategically-placed plant and area rugs to define the areas.

Q. I want to use the kitchen area in our flat as a dining place which would leave no space for appliances and storage cabinets. Can I shift the kitchen to the balcony? Keep in mind there is a sliding door linking the living room to the balcony.

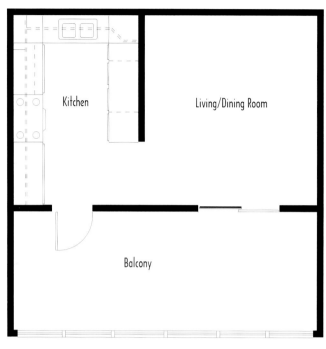

Before: **These cramped quarters didn't allow enough room for family dining.** ❧

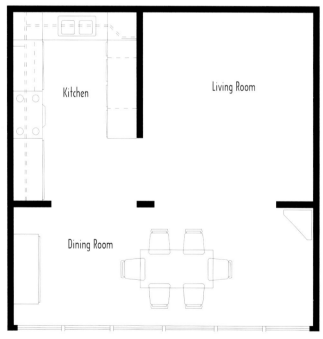

After: **A previously unused balcony was enclosed to create a separate dining area.** ❧

A. I assume you intend to enclose the balcony. You must also consider the cost of shifting the sink and adding plumbing, along with additional wiring required for the refrigerator. Why not make the balcony into a unique alfresco dining place instead?

Give the kitchen a wide open feeling with lots of light by removing the door to the balcony and replacing it with a large casement opening. Then close in the balcony with loads of big windows. A ceiling fan over the table helps to stir the air around and adds to the Casablanca ambience.

Remove the sliding door that links the living room to the new dining area. Replace it also with another over-sized casement opening. You probably will not be able to do away with the entire wall because it is most likely loadbearing.

Q. Our apartment doesn't have a dining room. How can I create an eating area in the kitchen that is separate from the work space?

A. A revival of glass blocks, which were last hot in the 1950s, have provided a new dimension to the concept of room dividers. They solve a multitude of problems and have so many pluses, the main one being an attractive way to separate space without getting a closed-in feeling. I needed something in our Bangalore home to divide the kitchen from the informal dining area and decided glass blocks were just the thing. I also needed more wall space in the kitchen area for a large refrigerator, so the glass

Glassed-in Privacy ▶
This stair-step glass wall is an opaque privacy wall (designed by the author) that separates a cosy eating area and the work space of a busy kitchen. The open space at the top of the partial wall allows for cross-ventilation.
Photo by Pallon Daruwala ❧

wall was the perfect answer for both problems. The result has been highly successful, and I freely recommend the idea. (***Photo on page 61***).

Q. Which is better for separating the kitchen from the dining area — a sliding door or a snack counter?

A. A sliding door that separates the two rooms allows for a more formal dining room setting. It's also a good idea if heavy-duty Indian/Asian cooking is the norm.

A snack counter opens everything up for a more casual living style. There's no hiding kitchen messes and cooking odours. But it's a great place for quick meals or breakfast for the kids. Another big plus is that the counter gives you extra work space and a place for the kids to colour and finger paint. The choice depends upon your personal needs.

Q. I hate eating in the living room, but we don't have a separate dining room. What's the best way to give the dining area an inviting look without overpowering the living room?

A. For starters, get a dining table and chairs that blend in style and colour with the living room furniture — notice I didn't say matching; blending is more interesting. Treat the whole space as a living room with a multipurpose table in it rather than a living/dining combo. A round or square table works best — guests seem to be drawn over to sit around them for chatting and elbow-bending as well as having a meal.

However, it isn't always practical to buy a new table just because the old one isn't the right shape. If this is the case, use what you have. In the ***photo on right***, interior designer Rosalie Chidwick ties her dining corner to the living room

area with theme and mood. The style of the table and chairs, the painting and the accessories are in harmony with the living room decor and, indeed, the whole flat.

If the total area is average-to-small in size, consider using a neutral colour scheme with accents in muted hues. The effect is low profile but nonetheless appealing.

Q. Our problem is a long, narrow combination dining room and living room that has a high ceiling. Should we raise the floor to get rid of this tall, skinny look? I don't

Blending In
This unobtrusive dining space at interior designer Rosalie Chidwick's flat takes up little more than a corner of her living/dining room combo. Since blending was her intent, she has done nothing to define the area and has even left off the usual area rug under the table.
Photo by Pallon Daruwala

know what else to do.

A. The high ceiling really isn't an insoluble problem. You can work with it by adding a couple of architectural details and adopting a daring approach to the use of colour. The idea is to trick the eye into believing that the room is correctly proportioned. Starting at the top and working downwards, here is what you can do: if you don't have crown moulding, add wide wooden mouldings all around the room. Position the mouldings so the top edges are about 10 to 15 cms (4 to 6 ins.) from the ceiling.

Moving down the wall, add wide mouldings (but not as wide as the mouldings next to the ceiling) to make a chair railing around the dining area. Nail the mouldings 76 to 92 cms (30 to 36 ins.) from the floor. Adding a wallpaper border that coordinates with the paint is an option. Patterns with fruit, flowers and the Greek or Chinese key design, to name a few, work well in dining areas. Install the border so that the bottom edge rests on the top of the new chair rail. You don't want any wall space showing between the border and the chair rail.

Now you are ready to work some visual miracles with paint. I know the concept of using colour on the ceiling is new to Asia, so going a step farther to suggest a darkish-coloured ceiling must be revolutionary. Please trust me on this one — the effect is outstanding. Paint the ceiling several shades darker than the colour you have selected for the walls. Continue the same shade of paint down the narrow strip of wall space above the mouldings. In effect, what this does is visually lower the ceiling to the bottom of the mouldings. Paint the mouldings the same shade as the ceiling, using a matte-finish enamel to subtly highlight this little detail.

You will need to paint the wall space between the mouldings and the chair rail a medium shade of the same colour as the ceiling. Again using a matte-finish enamel, paint the chair rail a bit lighter than the mouldings above. The wall below the chair rail will be lighter than the wall space above the chair rail. In short, the ceiling, the upper wall space and the bottom of the wall will be in graduating shades of the same colour.

Finally, paint the doors and all wood framing the same colour as the chair railing.

Do pictures and wall hangings in large groupings — the length must slightly exceed the height.

Angle the furniture placement instead of lining the pieces up along the long walls, and don't go for low, squatty furniture. Remember, the operative words are balance and proportion. Choose a round dining table and round accent tables in the living area. Too many straight lines are boring.

Rely on table and floor lamps for lighting the living area, and splurge on a super hanging light for the dining table.

Break up the long corridor look by separating the dining and living areas with a free-standing, mirrored screen. Mirrors are great for creating illusions.

Don't even think about raising the floor — that's not an option.

Q. We're planning to build our first home and needs lots of help. How much space is needed for a table in an eat-in kitchen?

A. All but the tiniest kitchens can hold a table of some sort. But, if you fancy an old-fashioned kitchen-table concept like that in Elaine Ghosh's bungalow (*page 64*), you will need more room. Measure the size of the desired table and chairs as though people were already seated and add at least 30 cms (12 ins.) behind each chair for manoeuvrability.

For small kitchens, consider a drop-leaf table that opens out at mealtime. Use folding chairs that stow away when not in use. Teeny-weeny kitchens can take a built-in, drop-down table which can also be used for extra work space when needed.

Dining In
A round table and armless side chairs that scoot under the table are space savers in Elaine Ghosh's eat-in kitchen. The terracotta floor, lovely wood cabinets and gleaming copper pots give her dining area lots of warm appeal. Photo by Pallon Daruwala ❧

Simply Fun
Push a square table
against the kitchen
wall — even a second-
hand card table will do,
place one or two
inexpensive chairs
parallel to the wall, add
a bright tablecloth and
some interesting
accessories and you've
got yourself a fun,
relaxing place to take
your meals.
Rendering
by Sheryl Perry 🏵

Richly Dressed
*A richly dressed buffet table is accessorised with droopy
imitation plants in a mile-high glass vase and gold papier-
mâché boxes with the ever-popular sun and star motif —
multi-coloured Kashmiri boxes are good too. Layers of
inexpensive sari fabric make an elegant table covering.*
Photo by the author ❧

Fresh Approach
*This mint-green and sparkling white colour combination is a
refreshing and modern way to decorate tables for anything
from a birthday party to a Christmas dinner. The centre
piece is made up of bleached twigs adorned with iridescent
balls tied on with narrow green bows. The whole thing is
stuck in a plain container which is all tied up in dark green
tissue paper. Reflective place mats are really pieces of
common kitchen aluminium wrap. Individual favours
are actually candles.* Photo by the author ❧

Q. I'm a bachelor, living alone for the first time, and I need some advice. I want a place to eat at in the kitchen because I hate eating at the dining table by myself. How can I do something that looks nice without spending much money?

A. If at all possible, I recommend a small table where you can sit down in a chair as opposed to a bar-stool placed at the counter top. There's something more satisfying about sitting at a table and having a meal. I always feel like I'm on-the-run when I have to eat at some type of counter, which is not quite the feeling you want at the end of a long day when you need to relax.

In the ***illustration on page 65***, you can see how one young man made a charming little dining spot for himself in his kitchen. By covering a not-so-good table with a colourful tablecloth and adding some zany accessories, a colour scheme and motif were established and carried out with the blue plastic folding chairs. Truly an economical solution to the problem.

Q. My husband is redoing a dining table and can't find veneer to match the wood. Any ideas?

A. If the table is an antique, you need to consult an expert. Otherwise, is it colour or grain that's important? If the wood is of similar hardness, you should be able to match up the new with the old by staining it.

TABLE DRESSING

Q. What is the secret of making a table look great?

A. I call "the secret" table dressing. Whether doing a romantic dinner for two, a buffet for the family or the gang from work, a well turned-out table is the beginning of a successful party. And table dressing can be fun and easy. However, it does take some vision and creativity. Or does it? There's nothing wrong with copying from the illustrations in this book and those in magazines for starters.

After a while you will want to do your own table designs. Here are some suggestions for the kind of materials you can use for decorations: choose from accessories you already have around the house (***photos opposite***). Add some colourful ribbons, candles, silk or fresh flowers, and fake greenery or real potted plants and you have the makings for some great decorations.

The beauty of using faux materials is that you can fix a table to last over long holidays such as Deepavali and Dussera. Fresh flowers are gorgeous, but they will eventually have to be replaced and that gets expensive. Save materials so you can build a supply of things to choose from. Change silk flowers to fit in with different themes and colour schemes by spray painting them gold, silver and other decorator colours. You can repaint them several times before they finally have to be pitched.

Q. I'm looking for something more in the way of dining room decorations for special occasions than the same old floral centrepiece flanked with a pair of candlesticks. What do you recommend?

Holiday Trimmings
Papier-mâché *angels,
sprayed with gold paint,
and greenery, interspersed
with flowers, nestle on a
red and gold silk Indian
shawl under a mass of
cascading ribbons. A red
sleeve covers the
chandelier chain and can be
changed to suit different
occasions and colour
schemes — a velcro seam
makes quick changes easy.*
Rendering
by Sheryl Perry ❧

A. Out-of-the-ordinary is always more appealing than the expected, and I love it! Even over-the-top is great for a change. The *illustration on the opposite page* is a rendering of the dining room of our Singapore bunglow, all decked out for the holidays. Masses of red and gold ribbons cascading from the chandelier, fake greenery and lots of big red candles filled up space in this over-sized room. The idea can be scaled down for smaller rooms. To decorate for different occasions like birthdays, anniversaries and graduations or to celebrate special events, change the ribbons and add real or silk flowers to the greenery for a festive look that decorates the dining room all day — not just at meal time.

P.S. Even the angels can be re-used for Valentine's Day decorations. I give them red candles to hold instead of gold and decorate their robes with little red hearts — so cute.❧

ENTERTAINING

Q. We would love to entertain our friends more often but find that it's getting very expensive as prices keep going up. How can we cut corners without seeming cheap?

A. Move away from the traditional way of doing meals with big spreads and umpteen choices. There are new, innovative ways to entertain that cost a lot less. Be the trendsetter in your group and the first to try out some of the following *avant-garde* ideas.

Try eating on the go at a progressive dinner. The latest rage in dining is great for apartment-style living. It goes like this — drinks and snacks at one flat, move on to another for the main course, and wind up the meal with dessert or fruit at the last place. This also works for neighbourhood parties and cities where traffic isn't a problem.

Another way to entertain is to call up a few people and organise a potluck dinner. Assign one person to bring a salad, someone else to do a vegetable and another for dessert. It is customary for the hostess to provide the meat dish. However, to keep the cost down you can share this responsibility with another person.

For something special, start a gourmet club with four couples that meet every month or two. Experiment with a different menu each time like Italian one month, regional Indian cuisine the next, then Shezwan Chinese and so on. Share expenses by doing this potluck style, too.

On the other hand, you don't have to feed your friends a whole meal every time you get together. Serve them coffee and dessert or wine and cheese and provide your own entertainment with a karaoke contest. Or, just do an after-dinner coffee party. Serve several different flavours like mocha, hazelnut and vanilla — coffee should be stronger than normal and served in smaller cups. Pretty little paper cups will do, especially when everyone wants to try several flavours. Set out shakers of cinnamon and chocolate powder for toppings.

Whether you try one or all of the above novel ways to toy with, keep the groups small. The *in* crowd are inviting fewer people at a time for more intimate parties.❧

Tip: Don't invest in an expensive ice chest. Use the kitchen sink to ice down cold drinks. No muss — no fuss. Pull the plug and the drippy mess goes down the drain.❧

CHAPTER 4

Kitchens

INTRODUCTION

In this era of servant-less households, kitchens have reverted to their earlier roles in history as the centres of family activities. Therefore, a movement is afoot to build bigger and more attractive kitchens, even in places where this room was previously most often tacked on to the rear of the house and treated like a necessary evil.

The changing attitude towards this work area is reflected in the universal interest in decorating the kitchen to make it an integral part of the house — an important room that family members and others are drawn to.

However, decorating is the last stage of kitchen planning. If you are lucky enough to have a clean slate to work with, either building a brand-new kitchen or renovating an old one, you must plan the layout first. If not, you can rely on relatively minor alterations and redecorating to establish the look and feel of your new family centre.

KITCHEN PLANNING

Kitchen projects start with planning. It is, after all, a workroom and must be designed for ease and efficiency. For the most step-saving layout, the three major appliances — sink, stove and refrigerator — must be positioned at the points of an imaginary triangle, called the *work triangle*[1]. The total distance around the triangle should measure between 366 cms (12 ft.) and 793 cms (26 ft.). This entails paying attention to plumbing and electrical installations so appliances can be placed in convenient locations.

There are three basic kitchen floor plans that allow for creating the work triangle. The **U-shaped layout** (*below left*) is frequently used in small, boxy kitchens. While it provides an ideal arrangement for one cook, when there are two or more people working at the same time they tend to get in each other's way. I once had a U-shaped kitchen that was so tiny I could stand in front of the sink, reach behind me to open the refrigerator with one hand and set a pot on the stove with the other hand. It was definitely a one-person kitchen! But a **U** that's too big is not good either because you run yourself to death moving from one appliance to the other. **The L-shaped layout** (*below centre*) is usually the most convenient, provided there is ample work space between the appliances — 91.5 to 105 cms (36 to 42 ins.). If there isn't, you'll waste time and energy getting to a usable counter top. **The galley-style layout** (*below right*) requires the least amount of space and is therefore a favourite for apartments. It is best suited for one cook.

While many designers have added a fourth layout by using the currently popular kitchen island as a point of

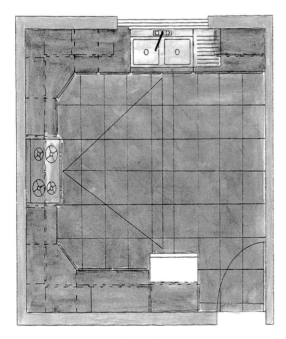

U-shaped layout

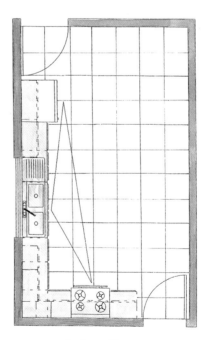

L-shaped layout

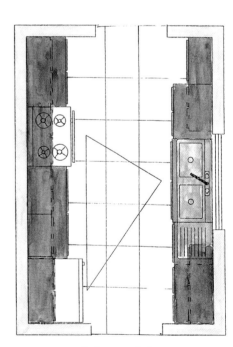

Gallery-style layout

---

1. The concept of the work triangle was developed by researchers at the University of Illinois, USA, in the early 1950s and has endured the test of time as the most functional kitchen layout.

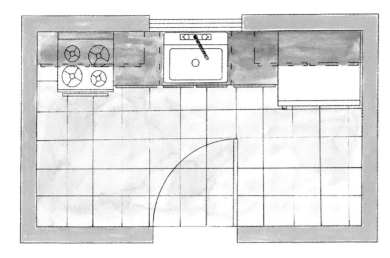

Single-wall Design

the work triangle, I have not included it. That's because I'm opposed to the idea of having a major cooking or cleaning-up zone in the middle of the room — for good reasons: sinks are where dirty glasses and cups pile up during the day. They become too obvious in the middle of the room, making an otherwise tidy kitchen look messy. Besides, there is no place for a backsplash on an island so water splatters onto the counter top and runs onto the floor.

Island cooking centres are impractical for the same reason. Without any protection behind the stove, grease and food splatter all over the place. And as I shall explain later in the chapter, cooker hoods are ineffective when placed in the middle of the room.

Another layout, called the single-wall design (*top*), is common for tiny kitchens. It is the least efficient of all the examples because it lacks the convenience of the work triangle. If you're stuck with this floor plan, make it work for you by positioning the sink in the centre and allowing at least 91.5 cms (36 ins.) of counter-top space on both sides.

Q. What are the rules about placing appliances?

A. The refrigerator should be at the end of the counter so it won't interrupt the flow of the work top with at least 61 to 91.5 cms (24 to 36 ins.) of counter space on one side. Be sure the refrigerator door opens in a convenient direction. Never place the refrigerator next to the cooker because the heat generated by the cooker effects the efficiency of the fridge.

Put the cooker 105 to 122 cms (42 to 48 ins.) from the opposite counter or wall so you will have room to open the oven door. There should be at least 46 to 61 cms (18 to 24 ins.) of free counter space on both sides of the cooker for work space. Don't place the cooker next to a door or window. The wind will play havoc with gas flames and even interferes with the effectiveness of electric burners. Also, cooker hoods and exhaust fans aren't as powerful as Mother Nature so odours and cooking grease will be blown throughout the house.

Refer to the kitchen layout drawings for ways to place appliances correctly.

Tip: For safety and convenience, the cook top should be dropped slightly lower than the counter top so you can see and tend the pots with less risk of burning yourself.

Q. I'm a novice at interior decorating and wonder why kitchen sinks are always placed at the window and not elsewhere?

A. I suppose kitchen designers think people like to have a view while they work at the sink. But if you'd rather stare at the wall, there's no reason why the sink can't be installed anywhere you want it, providing there is access to the plumbing and hot-water heater. Just be sure it's located within the work triangle — or you may later regret your attempt at being different.

Q. What's the latest trend in kitchen designs?

A. That depends upon your locality. In most places, the trend is towards more spacious floor plans designed with the latest appliances for ease and convenience. But, in some tropical areas where weather permits, there is a trend towards the double concept — wet and dry kitchens. The wet kitchen is where the heavy-duty cooking is done, and the dry kitchen is the big, fancy room where the less messy food is prepared. Unless you have staff, I think this fad is nonsense. What a lot of running back and forth this takes!

The double-concept idea is the result of impractically designed open or family-style kitchens that are more for show than for food preparation. That means the real cooking is moving outside and out of sight again. This is progress? I think not. A well-planned kitchen must, should and can meet all your family's needs.

There is one major exception: when a very tiny kitchen has been opened up for a particular reason and cooking space was sacrificed in the process. In this case, an adjacent balcony or patio makes a handy wet kitchen. And since the whole area is so small, no one is going to get worn out taking extra steps.

For the style conscious, some pre-built units are available with cabinets and enamelled doors under a stainless steel top and sink that are good for back kitchens. But usually wet kitchens are simply concrete or cinder blocks with the sink and cook top just set in. A wooden frame is built around the concrete to hold the doors. It's more cost effective than pre-build systems.

Or you can go super cheap with just a covered porch or utility area, a couple of gas burners, and a laundry sink for washing up big pots and *kadai*/woks.

Q. We want our new kitchen to be really up-to-date. What hot new features should we consider during the planning and costing stages?

A. The three most popular convenience features people in India and other economically growing Asian countries are turning to are microwave ovens, built-in or counter-top models; dishwashers for cleaner, germ-free dishes and faster tidying up; and the latest in cooker hoods for quieter and more effective action.

Tip: New Indian households should plan for the near future and purchase dishwasher-safe and microwave-proof cooking utensils.

Open Concept

Revolutionary ideas about kitchen design allow for more flexibility in using this room to suit the family's needs. For example, when we don't have the space for a huge kitchen-cum-family room, the open concept is now a popular option. The idea is to remove the wall between the kitchen and the dining-living room.

The cooking area is usually separated from the living area by a breakfast counter, which takes the place of the kitchen table. Personally, I find that this lined-up approach to eating lacks the friendliness of the old-fashioned kitchen table and should be avoided when space permits an alternative. But it is a solution for those who don't want to miss out on things while they prepare family meals and, also, for those who enjoy entertaining and don't want to be cooped up in the kitchen while their guests are having all the fun.

Q. While we like the idea of an open-plan kitchen for our new flat, we are afraid that the furniture and drapes in the living and dining areas will soak up cooking odours and that greasy dirt will stain them. Please advise.

A. You're smart to identify potential problems while the kitchen is still in the planning stages. The solution for cooking messes is an efficient cooker hood to carry grease and odours up and out of your flat. Every situation is different, and you need a specialist to recommend the best hood for your type of cooking and for the area it's expected to service. Bigger spaces require more power. For more on cooker hoods in this chapter, read on.

If there is a small utility balcony off the kitchen, you should consider a second cooking area to handle heavy-duty cooking. It doesn't have to be an elaborate setup. A couple of gas burners for *kadai/*wok cooking and a deep laundry sink for washing up will do.

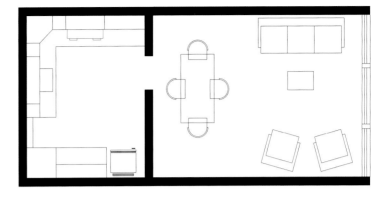

Original Layout

Q. I would really appreciate it if you could give me some idea how to extend the dining-living and kitchen areas of our new flat, and at the same time arrange the dining table in the hall as we prefer to enjoy our food while watching TV.

A. For a more open look, remove the common wall between the kitchen and dining-living room and put in a snack counter. This will also give you lots of extra counter-top work space and under-counter storage cabinets.

Go for a space-saving square dining table with a leaf for those times when you need a bigger table and stow the extra chairs in some other place. Choose a style that coordinates with the living room set. It can also double as a game table and a gathering place for drinks. Don't think of it as a dining table, but rather as a multi-purpose spot where you also take your meals. Put the TV on a swivel-top base for easy viewing from any direction.

Q. We hate feeling cooped up and wanted to pull down the wall between our kitchen and dining room. Now we've decided it's not practical because of the grease and cooking odours. Any suggestions?

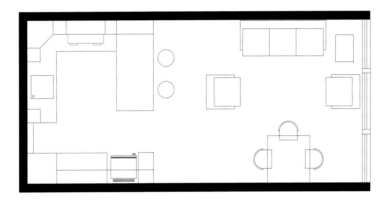

New Layout after Modifications

A. Make the opening between the rooms larger than normal to open things up when you want to. Have doors fitted so you can close off the kitchen when you're cooking so grease and odours don't float through the house. Use high quality, attractive double sliding or bi-fold doors — actually I prefer the latter since they don't take up wall space. The doors should be made of wood, either plain or decorative to suit your decorating theme. You can even get them made with frosted or stained glass insets to let in more light when they're closed.

COOKERS

Advertisements for all kinds of space-age cookers and cook tops are popping off the pages of decorating magazines. Some of the terminology sounds like something from "Future Watch". But, believe it or not, things such as halogen burners and magnetic induction cookers are on the market and have been available in some parts of Asia for several years. Read on for the low-down about what's going to be in the stores in the not-too-distant future.❧

Q. I see so many ads for ceramic cookers. What's the scoop, and are they practical for India?

A. These are cookers that have a flat, smooth top made out of a ceramic material. The heating elements are underneath the ceramic surface and hidden from view. They can be heated by gas burners, regular electric elements, high-speed radiant elements, or quartz-halogen elements. The high-speed radiant burners work like standard electric coils except the coils are placed below the ceramic top.

Flat-surfaced cooking tops are popular in Europe and very trendy in the US. Now, many people in Asia are looking at them because electricity is safer and cleaner than gas. You don't have to worry about the wind blowing out the flame, and it's easier to control the heat, an improvement over the old-style electric stove tops. A big plus is that ceramic tops are fast and simple to wipe off. No pieces and parts to scrub. They're good when you aren't using a *kadai*/wok.

On the down side, cooking techniques have to be adjusted and patience is needed to change over from old-style burners to this new kind of food preparation. You must be careful about the bottoms of your pots and pans. Too rough, and the ceramic surface gets scratched. Uneven or slightly warped, and the food won't cook evenly. Spills run all over the cabinet and onto the floor, which can be dangerous especially when babies and toddlers are around. Cooking on electric models is dicey in places that have fluctuating power and frequent outages. It's also much more expensive than gas.

You will need a separate *kadai*/wok burner for Indian/Asian cooking. Or you can go for an electric wok.

Q. What is halogen heat, and is it really so special?

A. Halogen works something like an incandescent light bulb. It glows red the instant you turn it on. The heat is spontaneous like gas. There's no waiting to warm up, so people who are used to cooking on gas go for it. Other plus features include more accurate control than traditional electric elements and better response straight away.

Minuses to watch for: it heats up so fast that it can be dangerous. You're likely to burn up some dinners and maybe some hot pads before you adjust to a new way of cooking.

Q. How do magnetic induction cookers work?

A. Heat is transferred through ceramic or glass tiles directly to speciality metallic cookware. Aluminium, glass and copper pots won't work. Heating is instantaneous and the surface stays cool like a microwave. They presently come in one-burner units and are very expensive.❧

Tip: Young, hi-tech devotees should select pots and pans made of enamel and cast iron that will work for induction cooking. Also, they will want cookware with very smooth bottoms so they won't scratch ceramic and glass cooking surfaces.❧

COOKER HOODS

Q. My grandmother got along just fine without all these hi-tech kitchen appliances like cooker hoods. Why do we need them these days?

A. In many parts of the world, kitchens were not a part of the main house in our grandmothers' day. Heat and unpleasant cooking odours made outdoor kitchens practical as well preferable. When changing times moved kitchens indoors, the old chimney concept that provided natural ventilation for cooking odours and oily messes was lost. It's no wonder kitchens have been shunted off to the backs of houses and other obscure places.

Now that modern living is making the kitchen a popular place to be after all, people go for cooker hoods of all types and prices to do the work of the old chimneys, which makes the kitchen more comfortable. But all too often, bad choices are made and the hood doesn't match up with the size of the kitchen and the kind of cooking it's expected to handle. The biggest problem is that cooker hoods frequently aren't installed properly, so they don't work right and grimy grease coats everything. The size of the ducting and its placement is most important for efficiency, noise level and the life of the motor.

Q. What does the cooker hood do?

A. Assuming the hood has a strong suction capacity, is the right size for the job, and all the pieces and parts are installed properly, you can expect it to remove up to 80 - 90% of the air-borne grease, odours, steam, and smoke. If you go for normal capacity, you get only 40% of the mess extracted and 60% goes back into the room.

Q. How does it work?

A. Basically there are two kinds of systems. The extraction system sucks up stuff, routes it through a filter and either directly or eventually expels it into the open air, via ducting, chimneys or recirculation. The recirculating system carries cooking fumes through a series of filters and returns them to the kitchen, theoretically clean and free of smells.

It goes without saying that the extraction system will give the best results, but sometimes the structural layout prevents that type of installation. When there is no alternative, a recirculating system is better than nothing, but it won't handle Indian/Asian cooking.

Q. Should the venting go through the ceiling or the wall?

A. The ideal location for the stove and hood are on an outside wall so the hood can be vented straight out with no ducting required. Next best is a dropped ceiling with ducting routed the shortest possible distance with few, or better yet, no turns.

Q. Are charcoal filters any good?

A. Charcoal filters are not necessary if the hood is properly ducted to the outside. It will actually block air flow to the outside as it's another barrier. Now there are more effective filtering operations that go with different types and brands of hoods. And many of the filters can be washed in a dishwasher.

Q. When should filters be cleaned?

A. Clean filters regularly. The average for Indian/Asian cooking is once every two weeks. Lots of heavy-duty cooking requires more frequent cleaning. The cleaner the filter, the better it works.

Q. Does Indian/Asian cooking require industrial-sized cooker hoods? What about just regular cooking?

A. Unless your family is the size of a small army or you're thinking of opening a restaurant, an industrial hood is overkill for home use. They have a different grease filter, larger motor, larger ducting, and no speed controls. They are normally very noisy, so it's best to house the motor outside.

A heavy-duty hood with a strong motor and external exhaust that suits the size of the kitchen and the location of the cooking centre is what you should have. Call in some product specialists to assess your needs and give you estimates.

Q. What does it cost to operate a cooker hood and how long will it last?

A. Even the largest cooker hood uses less than 400 watts of electricity or one-fifth the amount of that used for an electric kettle. So operating costs really aren't a factor. They're usually designed to last up to 10,000 hours of use.

Q. How do you arrange the kitchen to get the most from the cooker hood?

A. Try to design the kitchen so the cooking area is not in the way of wind and drafty areas. If it's next to an open window, the best won't be enough. Drafts from the window will be stronger than the suction of any hood. In trendy central island cooking, you cannot expect the hood to work efficiently because of the air circulation around the hood.

Q. Are normal room-exhaust fans effective in the kitchen?

A. Well, they are better than nothing. If that's your only choice, be sure to install the fan very near the stove in order to do any good at all.

DECORATING

If you're building or renovating and have chosen a floor plan, selected your appliances and positioned them, it's time to turn your attention to the decorating process. If you're just redecorating, you can get right down to the fun part.

Decorating doesn't have to be an expensive project. It just takes a little imagination. To get the creative juices flowing, scan the decorating magazines. Pull out the appealing pictures and create a reference folder. You will soon see a pattern forming that will help you decide on the mood and the look or theme you want to create.

After you determine what suits you, dig around in your cupboards for attractive containers to hold wooden spoons and cooking utensils: common terracotta pots for a garden theme, brushed aluminium or stainless steel beakers for hi-tech, a wacky pitcher for mod. Got any old canisters around? Just about anything will work, except plastic — it's not ecofriendly.

Pay attention to your window treatment unless the window makes a statement on its own, which doesn't happen very often. Any old curtain won't do the trick. In a garden setting use a simple *chik*; hi-tech and contemporary decor scream for metallic mini blinds. (**For more window ideas, read Chapter 8.**)

Hang some pictures or posters that fit your motif. Add some green plants in cheerful pots to your window sill. Have fun! That's really what decorating is all about.

Q. We're hooked on the country look and want it for our old kitchen, but we can't afford renovations. What to do?

Cooking Country Style
Using her lively imagination and wonderful sense of what works, Melinda Alexander transformed an uninteresting bungalow kitchen into a cosy country delight. The look and feeling were achieved with cosmetic decorating —
paint, a wallpaper border and accessories.
Rendering by
Sheryl Perry🍂

S. PERRY '97

A. Don't worry; it's easy! You can get the results you want by using some simple decorating techniques that won't cost too much money.

While country-styled kitchens are regularly featured in most every decorating magazine, they are usually sophisticated versions that scream, "Done by a decorator!" There's also a stereotyped sameness about them which is not what you want. The country look should be unpretentious, inviting and accessorised with simple everyday items made out of natural materials. Above all, it must ooze personality.

Old bungalow-style kitchens are particularly suited to the look and take very little dressing up to get the effect you want. For example, check out the **illustration on page 79** that shows how Melinda Alexander focused on the country look for her formerly lack-lustre kitchen. The idea is carried out with barnyard animals on the hanging wrought iron rack, blue and white checked curtains, some clever accessories, lots of wicker baskets, and a wallpaper border with a chicken motif. The result is very down-home, cosy country.

Q. I'm very keen on having a rustic look for the kitchen. How do I achieve it?

A. The rustic look that's so popular in Europe and America uses lots of natural materials like timber beams, brick or stone for flooring and even accent walls, and wood cabinets. The colour scheme is usually in earth-related tones. The result is a very heavy, dark feeling that harkens back to peasant farms and pioneer days when rough and rugged was all they had. In its purest form, I don't think the look is practical for some parts of the world.

Never mind. You can simulate the look instead of copying it and still get the effect you want, which I assume is a simple, warm and cosy atmosphere. Elaine Ghosh did just that in her lovely kitchen (**photo opposite**).

Go for rich wood tones, natural or knotty pine cabinets.

Use ceramic tile that looks like brick or stone for the floors and counter tops. The colour scheme should be muted earth tones that aren't quite so drab.

Accessorise with brass and copper pots hung on the wall or from a suspended rack. Keep the windows bare or at least very simple — they weren't into window dressing in the old days. If there's space for furniture, get a wood-plank table with benches and a free-standing cupboard to display stone crockery. The idea is to keep it plain to avoid a contrived look that comes with trying too hard.❧

Colour Schemes

A word of caution on choosing kitchen colour schemes: remember that fad colours go out of fashion and date your room. Although it is currently trendy to do a 50s or 60s style, stick to white or off-white appliances for versatile best-buys. Set your theme with paint, window treatments and accessories, which are relatively cheap to change. Replacing wall tiles and flooring are messy and expensive projects so go for non-obtrusive background colours that are easy to work around.

The colour combinations you choose are largely a matter of personal choice. However, there are some guidelines to help you decide. For starters, if your kitchen is an open concept design, you should coordinate the colours with the rest of the open area. If not, you have more freedom to do something different. As always when faced with making colour choices, I recommend visiting several fabric stores and looking at bolts and bolts of different patterned

Dressed-up Country ▶
Elaine Ghosh established her own version of chic rustic in a Bangalore kitchen. Rich wood cabinetry and the gleaming terracotta tile floor provide the natural elements. Her large collection of copper pots and utensils are the only decorations.
Photo by Pallon Daruwala ❧

fabrics. When you find some that you really like, buy at least one-half metre. Take them home with you and tape them to the kitchen wall or the cabinet doors. After you look at them for awhile, you'll find out which colour combinations you feel comfortable with. If you decide on earthy tones, just think about Mother Nature's colour palette — she seldom makes any mistakes.❧

Q. Please help me with some colour choices. What colour should I pick for kitchen cabinets to go with peachy coloured tiles? I want something that makes the kitchen feel spacious and bright.

A. While you may not think of grey as a lively colour, the right shade works and is great with peach. A very soft dove-grey or swansdown will really open up the room. Paint the trim a brighter shade of peach than the tile, but don't get fluorescent. The result is a 50s look.

For something jazzier and more up-to-date, team up peach with bright dark blue or forest green. Or for sheer drama, use charcoal grey with peach and go to a darker peach for the trim.

Q. I'm thinking about getting wood cabinets, stained to match the brown ceramic tile, but I'm afraid it will close up the room even more. What do you suggest?

A. I think a relatively dark monochromatic colour scheme will make the kitchen seem cramped and boring. For

◀ *Tribal Inspiration*
May Kottukapally-Demann's cheerful kitchen is decorated in her favourite tribal motif. Open shelving shows off her pottery and keeps her cookbook collection within easy reach. The over-sized checkerboard tiles makes the walls look bigger than they actually are. Photo by Pallon Daruwala ❧

something bright and new looking, go for cabinets in a very light shade of wood such as natural or white pine. This gives you all kinds of leeway for choosing a decorating theme and for selecting accent colours.

Q. Although my kitchen is somewhat small, I want to make it really interesting. What can I do?

A. You can make even the smallest kitchen ooze with personality and charm by stretching your imagination. Here are a few ideas from my friend, May Kottukapally-Demann, who used colour and technique fearlessly to create a setting that's guaranteed to bring smiles of pleasure to all who enter (**photos opposite and on page 84**). She carried the tribal theme of her home right into the kitchen, where the walls are hand painted with bright folk art.

Some of the wooden cabinet frames were enhanced with Rajasthani doors while others were left uncovered to expose open shelving for display. For extra storage May placed a tribal chest in a space next to a built-in unit. Her unique ability to turn the ordinary into the *extraordinaire* is an inspiration to us all.

Q. We have huge ugly pipes standing from floor to ceiling in the corner of the kitchen. We can't afford to box it in, so we're thinking about painting it an attractive colour. What's the best way to go?

A. I've seen some neat things done in both kitchens and bathrooms where the pipes were painted to purposely stand out as accents. For example, shiny black or Chinese red against white walls in a black and white colour scheme works for hi-tech, modern and funky looks.

Alternately, in a more conservative situation, when you don't want to emphasize the pipes, paint them to match the wall and they will disappear. Well, not completely, but they will blend in and not look so obvious.

Q. What's the best way to make a small kitchen look bigger?

A. Creating the visual effect of space in a small kitchen is most important. Of course, we all know that white is the traditional colour for making small rooms appear larger. And it's always been a favourite colour for kitchens because there's something sanitary about white. If that's your choice, be sure to add an accent colour to keep it from looking too clinical. But stick to a limited colour scheme so it's not overpowering.

Use one or two different shades for tiles, flooring, walls, and accessories for the best results. But you have other choices that will work just as well. You can go for a sand colour that's great with pine cabinets and cabinets with natural finishes. Neutrals like dove-grey are also very good and very *in* right now. Or shades of white like cream or a white with a pinkish cast for warmth or go cool with a bluish white or apple-white which has a greenish cast.

Then liven things up with an accent colour in brighter tones of the same shade. For example, emerald green would be smashing with apple-green, sunshine yellow with old ivory, terracotta with pinkish white, and so on.

For a clean flowing line your appliances should match the cabinets. And kitchen sinks should be similar to the colour of the work top.

◄ *Kitchen Art*
Handpainted folk art and handicrafts
decorate May Kottukapally-Demann's walls above a
free-standing storage chest. A piece of woven textile,
draped over a simple curtain rod, makes a colourful
and well-coordinated window treatment.
Photo by Pallon Daruwala ❧

Q. How can I make a derelict storage area between the kitchen and dining room of our old bungalow look attractive? I think it was called a butler's pantry in the old days.

A. They still are called butler's pantries, and there has been a revival in their popularity in new homes. They can be treated several ways: it can be a transitional space between the two rooms with decorations that reflect both; it can copy the decor of the dining room; or as in the case of Melinda Alexander's preference, it can duplicate the motif of the kitchen. Melinda's bungalow had a lacklustre butler's pantry, much as you describe, that she turned into a picturesque addition to her country kitchen (*photo on page 87*).❧

Tiling

Q. I've had the kitchen repainted and now the border on the wall tiles doesn't go. What can be done? We really can't afford to change it all out.

A. The experts tell me you can either paint the border or cover it up with a self-sticking wallpaper border. Check the paint stores for a durable epoxy paint that covers ceramic tile. The surface must be absolutely clean and grease free before application. It may be worth trying before you go to the expense of replacing the tiles. I'd think twice about having the border chipped out. It takes a very skilled workman with the proper electric tools to do the job without damaging the rest of the tiles.

Q. I'm so tired of the same old plain kitchen tiling. Isn't there something more imaginative happening these days?

A. The big look in tile is mixing up all sizes and colours to create interesting patterns and designs. Take a clue from the over-sized tiling done in a checkerboard mosaic pattern in the *photo on page 82,* which is relatively easy to install. A more complicated design takes careful planning and is more difficult to install correctly. If you decide on a variety of tiles of different sizes and thicknesses, be sure the finished surface is smooth and flat. The effect can be ruined with sloppy workmanship.❧

Floors

A word about kitchen floors: first and foremost, they must be practical. Much of the natural flooring materials currently in vogue in the West, such as wood and brick or stone, just don't work in heavy-duty kitchens. Even marble has its drawbacks because it's porous and stains are unavoidable. On the other hand, white marble is manageable because you can use cleaning agents that contain bleach — I speak from experience.

All things considered, it's hard to beat a good quality ceramic tile for durability and cleanliness as well as style. The key word here is Quality. Flooring is expensive to replace so do it right the first time.

The following query exemplifies my point. I rest my case.

Q. What can be done about a once-beautiful slate kitchen floor that is now covered with a layer of tacky grease?

A. If you use porous materials and like the look, you just have to be prepared to put up with inconveniences like grease-caked floors. Obviously, such flooring requires frequent and vigorous scrubbing so the grease doesn't get a chance to settle in. And you can't stop there — you have to rinse the floor thoroughly. Even though the cleaning product may not require rinsing, a sticky residue will accumulate if you don't. A coating of polyurethane helps seal up porous materials, but nothing less than the best will work and even that scratches in heavy trafficked areas.❧

CABINETS AND WORK TOPS

My pet peeve is that most kitchen cabinets and storage units are ill-conceived and poorly placed. What's so special about the blank space between the tops of the cabinets and the ceiling that we have to look at it? Why isn't this precious space used for more cupboards? Why aren't cabinets over the refrigerator *de rigueur?* What's wrong with putting a cabinet over the door? And why are designers so crazy about putting open shelving in the messiest room in the house? Because contractors don't think of these possibilities and designers are more concerned with aesthetics than practicality, that's why.❧

Q. The ugly hot-water geyser and water filter ruin the looks of my kitchen. What's a good solution?

A. That's two separate problems, but both of these unsightly necessities can be enclosed. Have a cupboard built for the geyser that has a fire-proof lining and louvered doors for ventilation. To insure safety and conserve energy, turn off the geyser when you're out for the day, at night after the cleanup chores are done, and when you're on holiday.

An ordinary cabinet can be built around the water filter (*photo on page 88*). Just be sure to leave enough space to get the pitcher under the spout. To avoid flooding accidents, turn off the filter when you aren't using it — you never know when the thing might malfunction.

Q. I can't stand the kitchen cabinets that came with our new apartment. Tearing them all out will damage the wall tiles and flooring and end up costing a fortune. Help!

A. Don't panic — there's an easier way to tackle this problem. Just change out the cabinet doors and hardware

Blue and White Stowaway
This butler's pantry is now a charming spot with a country-style motif that matches Melinda Alexander's kitchen. Photo by Peter Mealin

(door handles and drawer pulls) to get maximum effect for minimum cost. Do your homework by scanning decorator magazines to find a style you like and get a good carpenter to copy it. If your cabinets are standard units, there's a wide range of ready-made styles and colour combinations to choose from.

If you don't like the colour of the frame, you can paint, revarnish or laminate it to work in with the new doors. I used laminate in one of my own kitchens and loved the new look.

Q. The dark laminated cabinets that go all around the kitchen walls are awful. What can be done to brighten up this small dreary-looking kitchen without giving up the storage space?

A. Don't even think about ripping out valuable storage cabinets just because you don't like their looks. It's too easy to change their appearance by trying some of the ideas I've already suggested.

To open up a small gloomy kitchen, put glass doors on some of the top cabinets. Paint the insides a bright colour that coordinates with the frame. The treatment gives added dimension and a lot of interest to an otherwise boring kitchen. It's okay to mix things up by leaving regular doors on the cabinets that hold the messy items.

Q. I would like to use two different colours for my cabinets. What colour combination would be ideal for maintenance and eye-appeal? Should I change the floor to match the cabinets?

◄ **Deluxe Coverup**
Who would guess that the builder of this deluxe dream kitchen plopped an unsightly water purifier on a previously bare wall above the dishwasher? However, the clever lady of the house had a matching upper cabinet unit installed to cover the uglies and picked up some extra cabinet space in the process. Photo by Pallon Daruwala ❧

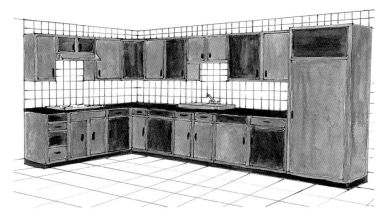

Randomly mixed two-colour cabinet doors and drawers work well in a small kitchen if the surrounds are simple. White ceramic-tile walls and floor are the best background to show off the novel colour scheme. ❧

A. You can use a two- or even a three-colour combination for doors and drawers. Make the frames of the wall cabinets and the base cabinets the same colour and randomly mix the accent colours on the doors top and bottom.

I have also seen kitchens with the wall cabinets done in one colour and the base units done in another. Usually the base units are varnished wood, and the frames of the wall cabinets are painted with an antique finish. The upper door frames are done to match the frame and have glass panels. To make this special effect work, you need a big kitchen because it comes off as a mishmash in a small one.

The determining factor in keeping cabinets clean is the material they are made from rather than colour. On certain surfaces, handprints and grease spots even show up on black. Matte finishes are harder to keep clean than high glosses.

Whether or not you decide to change your floor tiles depends upon the colour scheme you choose. But I wouldn't change them to match the floor to the cabinets. You'll end up overdoing a good idea, and your beautiful new cabinets would get lost in the shuffle. Read the section on selecting kitchen floors for some good, basic advice.

Q. Can laminated work tops really take the heat from hot pans right off the stove?

A. In a word, "No." Heavy duty ceramic tile can't take red-hot pans either, and extreme heat will leave a white mark on granite too. But why take the chance when there are so many cleverly designed hot pads and trivets around? Hang some close to the stove for convenience so you'll get into the habit of grabbing one before you reach for a pot.

Beware of trivets with holes or cut-out designs though. I made the mistake of putting a hot dish on one shaped like a pretty butterfly — the heat poured through the holes and damaged the finish on our dining table.

Q. I love the idea of marble or granite counter tops, but it's too expensive for our pocketbook. What's a good alternative?

A. Go for ceramic tiles that have the marbleised look you want — there's so much to choose from these days. Use easy-to-clean smooth-surfaced tiles with a semi-gloss or matte finish because scratches show up on shiny tiling. Please keep in mind that white grouting is impossible to keep clean, so tint the grouting to match or contrast with the tiles.❧

Creating Space

Q. To make the kitchen bigger, should I knock down the wall between the kitchen and the adjacent store room?

A. That depends upon your personal needs. If you need storage space for big items like the vacuum cleaner, suitcases and golf clubs, it's hard to do without a store room. However, if your family likes to hang out in the kitchen or you love to cook and need more cabinets and work space, knock out the walls. You will have the luxury of a big kitchen and probably enough room for an informal eating area. Either way a good kitchen

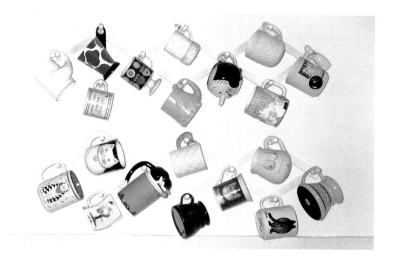

Accordion-like racks, painted white, blend into the white wall to show off the colourful mugs. Photo by the author ❧

planner can help you make the most of the available space.

Q. My kitchen is getting smaller. There is no more room to put anything and very little work space. Help!

A. More than likely you've managed to accumulate a bunch of things you don't need. Or at least things you don't need in the kitchen. Obviously, the first thing that has to be done is to clear out the clutter — both inside and outside the cabinets. To make room in overstuffed cabinets, remove seldom used items like party trays and extra-large pots that you need only occasionally for family get-togethers. If you can't find any place else, stow them in a box under a bed. Don't forget about using the tops of your wall-hung cabinets for things like baskets and large pottery pieces that you want to show off.

Look for alternative storage methods that also add a bit of dash. Use every inch of available space wisely. Hang pots and things from a pegboard over the stove or suspend a decorative rack for pans from the ceiling. Stuff a basket with cooking utensils to free up a drawer. Hang coffee mugs on the wall (**photo above**) and use stack caddies for glasses and small items. Invest in a wall-hung spice rack to get rid of all those messy little bottles that keep falling over anyway. Store crockery in the dining room and use a nearby closet as a pantry.

Now, organise all that cabinet space you've created. Buy rubberised-wire utility racks to hang on the inside of cabinet doors, especially under the sink for paraphernalia like sponges, brushes and scrubbers. Also, caddies under the sink are a necessity to keep cleaning aids in order.

Messy counter tops are not helpful for good work habits. They slow you down too. Throw out everything that isn't absolutely an essential part of your life. Clear away appliances. If it isn't something you use every single day — and I don't mean something you **might** use — put it inside the cabinet, on a shelf or in the pantry. Just get it off the counter top and preferably out of sight.

Add shelving wherever it makes sense. You can make a nice-looking bookshelf for your cookbooks so they're handy but not cluttering up valuable space. If you have to, you can also store small appliances on a shelf. But you should cover them up so they don't get yukky from kitchen grease. You can get some very decorative covers for things like toasters and mixers that are easy to wash. Add shelves over the windows and doors if possible. Another space saver that's nice if you have room is a utility trolley that you can wheel over to the closest outlet. Or put canisters and storage jars that hold flour, sugar and other staples on it so that you can move it around to anywhere you need it when you're cooking and baking.

Q. How can I put an island in my small kitchen to get more work space?

A. You don't want to build anything permanent in the middle of the floor if you don't have enough space to move around it. But here's a way to have your cake and eat it too. For those times when you need extra counter space for chopping and mixing, you can get a portable island with a chopping-block top. They come with wheels so you can move it around — even out to the balcony or patio to be close to the barbecue grill. ❧

Solving Everyday Problems

Q. I'm worried about the lead content in cheap crockery. I'd like to use them for everyday, but are they safe?

A. Bad news, dear reader. In many places there are no compulsory checks on the lead content in cheap, locally made or imported crockery.

Q. How do you handle washing up big kadai/woks that don't fit in prefab sinks?

A. Locally made and imported custom-sized sinks to suit every need are available. They come deep enough to wash the biggest *kadai*/wok. Alternately, but not as glamorous, a laundry sink can do up the job for much less. Cheaper yet, why not try using a smaller *kadai*/wok?

Q. How do you keep from getting drenched with water splashing everywhere when you wash dishes?

A. Get a new water tap with a pull-out spray and a deeper sink. The angle of the tap is most important. That's why goose-neck taps which point straight down are so good. Maybe your water pressure is too strong, and you need a fixture with settings for hard and soft flow so you don't get soaked. Sometimes the problem is in the dishwashing technique. Don't hold the dishes too near the tap. Rinse the dishes in the sink so splashes go down the drain instead of on the front of your dress. ❧

CHAPTER 5

Bedrooms

INTRODUCTION

Once upon a time bedrooms were places where you came back to roost after a hard day's work. No one cared what it looked like as long as the bed was comfortable and the sheets were clean. But times have changed.

These days when space is so precious, people want more out of their bedrooms. They see them as retreats — private places for quiet getaways. Bedrooms are expected to be restful and different, and most importantly, they must look absolutely sensational.

If your bedroom is boringly ordinary, you are out of step with today's trends. Get with it and create your own special space to suit your feelings and your needs. Develop a mood-setting dream theme to live out your wildest fantasies. Do your bedroom up any way you want it — sail away to some exotic port-of-call or relax in the soft luxury of a feather duvet[1] and mounds of pillows. With today's vast array of bed linen to choose from, it's never been easier (*photo on page 94*).

In the old days sheets came only in plain white and were purely functional. Now, bed linen is a major part of the decorating scheme. And it doesn't stop there. You can finish off the whole room in no time by using coordinated accessories that range from curtains to lamp shades and waste baskets.

Since the bed is the biggest and most important thing in the room, it is the natural place to start. Dress it to the hilt. Pile on the pillows, mix and match the sheets and top it all off with a coordinated duvet or comforter[2]. Add a bed skirt[3] when the look you want calls for it.

---

1. Duvet: consists of two parts — a fluffy quilt, usually filled with eider down or synthetic stuffing which is inserted into a removable cover.

2. Comforter: a bulky quilt.

3. Bed skirt/bed valance (British term)/dust ruffle (American term): literally, a skirting that covers the blank space between the mattress set and the floor. A great cover-up for those things one shoves under the bed when storage space is limited.

On the other hand, if you hate all those pillows and think that kind of dressing is overkill, go for the more modest rustic[1] look. Or maybe the lean and simplistic lines of colonial or Shaker[2] are better still.

Take your pick for whatever suits you best — there's plenty to choose from. Department stores and specialty shops have a tempting array.

What's the *in* look? Everything from sentimental patterns to lavishly rich Oriental motifs and new, crisp yuppie designs. But the end result must always be romance, romance, romance, done with style and panache.

The decor should make a strong colour statement whether it's the purest whites, softest neutrals or the most voluptuous reds. Wimpy, washed-out pastels just aren't up to the mark any more and insipid-looking flowers are out. Floral patterns are punchy with clearer and brighter colours like oil paintings from Down Under (Australia) and splashy Monets.

But the biggest thing going are the Indian-inspired patterns. Mouth-watering hot and spicy colours introduce a whole new attitude about what's right for the bedroom (***photo on page 96***).

The bottom line is that people are no longer satisfied with making do or fixing up trendy little bedrooms. We're

◀ *Soft Landings*
A bed layered in exquisite Battenberg lace pillows, sheets and a feather duvet makes this bedroom a comfortable haven for repose. Photo by Pallon Daruwala

into high fashion these days — Big Time!

The perfect bedroom has it all. It's a multipurpose room that provides a comfortable place for sleeping and a private sanctuary for relaxing, reading and working with enough space for everything — including an *en suite* bathroom.

While most of us have to make do with less than the ultimate, we can go all out to make the bedroom the most personally appealing room in the house. Let's start with the essentials and eventually work our way towards the glamorous.

THE BASICS

Q. There are so many different sizes and types of mattresses that I'm quite confused. What should I look for?

A. Start by choosing a bed frame that's big enough to suit the comfort of whoever is going to sleep in it. Then go for the mattress, which in India is often custom-made to fit the bed. However, readymade mattress sets (mattress and foundation) are now available in India, and although they are expensive, they are catching on at the high end of the market.

To determine the most suitable fibre content and thickness, you must try it out. That means, find a mattress already made up like the one you're considering and lie down on it. Otherwise you will never know until it's too late

---

1. Rustic: a back-to-the-basics look. Bed coverings will be unfussy like a patchwork quilt or a simple Indian-style throw. Colours are often muted earthy tones, relating to Mother Nature. Review *Chapter 1* for more on themes and colours.

2. Shaker: a utilitarian and functional style not meant to be decorative. Originally everything was hand-made by a no-frills religious group called Shakers in England during the mid-18th century. Many immigrated to the USA, and now Shaker communities probably do not exist outside of America, and even that number is dwindling. But the Shaker look lives on and is currently enjoying great popularity because it blends in so well with other furniture styles.

Elephants on Parade
A beautiful antique Colonial
four-poster, swathed in
white netting, is topped off
with richly coloured fabrics
bearing Indian motifs.
Interior designer Rosalie
Chidwick uses a
look that's wildly popular in
the West right here at its
origin — in India.
Photo by
Rosalie Chidwick

whether or not the mattress is comfortable for you.

"Don't get bogged down in hype about degrees of firmness and construction," advises a Singapore-based orthopaedic surgeon. He tells his patients to make selections based on good support and comfort — after that, it's a matter of personal preference and budget.

In many other parts of Asia, and certainly in the West, readymade bedding is the norm. The options and price ranges are mindboggling. Shop around and try them out. Then select a mattress and foundation (sometimes called a divan set) that supports the body at all points. The foundation acts as a shock absorber to the mattress, so the two pieces should always be bought as a set.

To stretch the lifetime of your purchase, regardless of its type and material, you must flip the mattress and foundation end to end and turn it over three or four times a year. This also insures even wear and tear.

Tip: Sizes may vary, but generally a single mattress is .9 x 1.9 metres (3 x 6 ft. 3 ins.); a queen is 1.5 x 1.9 to 2 metres (5 x 6 ft. 3 to 6 ins.); and a king is 1.8 x 1.9 to 2 metres (6 x 6 ft. 3 to 6 ins.). Check your measurements before you go to shop for linen.

Q. Are cheap pillows okay to use or must I spend more to get a good one?

A. Simple guidelines for what's what in good pillows: if it's not comfortable, don't use it; and whatever you do, keep it clean. Frequent fluffing and airing will keep your favourite pillow free of sweaty odours and make it last longer.

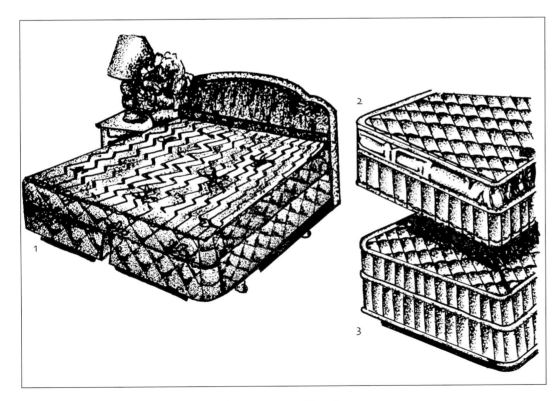

Mattress sets: 1. king size, 2. double, 3. single.

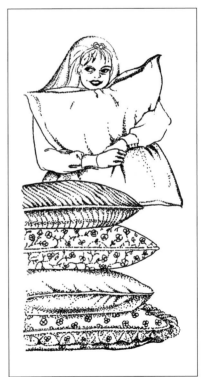

Selecting a comfortable pillow is a matter of personal taste.

Feather and down-filled pillows are the softest and the most natural-feeling. But polyester, hollow-fibre filled pillows are also fluffy and comfortable. Foam rubber isn't as soft and the material doesn't last as long.

If you are bothered by allergies, check out the labels for hypo-allergenic materials — especially cotton-filled pillows that have a great natural feather feel.

Q. I love fancy bed linen but find it too expensive for our budget. What to do?

A. Buy some ordinary pillow covers and decorate them yourself. Needlework is becoming a fashionable hobby again. If you are a beginner in the craft, start with something simple that you can finish quickly so you won't get bored or discouraged. You can embroider designs across one end of the pillow covers, using thread colours that coordinate with the bed linen or for a very elegant look, use tone-on-tone[1] thread. Classic white embroidery on white fabric is especially beautiful with lace added around the edges of the pillow covers.

This do-it-yourself concept can be carried a step further. After you complete the pillow covers, you may want to do the edge of the top sheet as well.

Q. Much emphasis is being put on the thread count of sheets. What is it and why is it important?

A. Thread count is the number of threads per square inch. For example, a sheet with a thread count of 200 has just that — 200 threads per square inch. The higher the number, the better for softness and durability.

Q. There are so many different kinds of sheets on the shelves these days, how do I know which ones are best?

A. The bedding industry continues to woo us as everybody, including high-fashion designers, jumps on the bandwagon. However, your choice must be governed by personal taste, your budget and some knowledge about what you're buying.

Most people who can afford them want 100% cotton bed linen with a high thread count because they have a cool, silky feeling. The ultimate are 100% cotton sateen[2] bed linen with a 250 to 340 thread count. As the name implies, sateen has a sheen to the finish that feels sensuous and luxurious next to the skin.

There's a wider colour and design range to choose from in 50% cotton to 50% polyester blends. Blended fabrics are easier to care for, dry faster, last longer, and are cheaper. But the picture is changing due to the back-to-nature movement and improved, no-iron cotton finishes.

Colour preferences are changing too. Traditionally solid whites, neutrals and pastels were popular and considered safe decorating choices. Now customers are reaching for bolder, more dramatic colours and more daring designs.

It's a mix and match, anything goes era. Matched packaged sets used to be the norm, but today people put together their own combinations. It's a more cost effective approach when you buy bottom sheets that go with a variety of pillow cases, quilts and duvets. Broken sets are frequently found on sale, which is another big plus for mixing it up.

---

1. Tone-on-tone: decoration is the same colour as the background.

2. Do not confuse cotton sateen with satin which is made out of silk or synthetic fibres.

Tip: Buyer beware! Sheet sizes vary according to manufacturer. Measure your mattress for length, width and thickness before you go shopping.

Q. What's the big deal about fitted bottom sheets?

A. Although fitted bottom sheets are *de rigueur* in the USA, they still haven't caught on in many parts of the world. The best argument I can give you in favour of fitted bottom sheets is that beds are easier to make up and stay neater. But a lot of people prefer to keep things simple and just use a flat sheet on the bottom — one reason is because of the various and confusing sizes of mattresses.

Tip: While top sheets aren't used in some places, they should be considered an option for a light coverup during hot weather.

A fitted bedcover is an easy way to keep a neat looking bed. However, it's expensive to buy and to maintain.

Q. Why aren't more people using formal bedcovers anymore? They looked so neat and tidy.

A. The main reason is simple economics. You won't see as many formal bedcovers being used in average homes anymore because they're expensive initially and most require dry cleaning. Also you can't use a fancy bedcover to keep warm so you have to buy at least a blanket or two as well.

Duvets and comforters are very popular because the casual look is *in*, and because they're cheaper — you can have two or three for the price of a fancy bedcover. Some are reversible so you get two for the price of one. And most are washable. In addition, you can quickly dress the bed with them during the day and cover up with them at night — another two-in-one benefit.

If you like the more formal mood of a traditional bedcover and can afford the luxury, go for it. A custom-made fitted cover (**bottom left**) will give the tidy appearance you crave and is easier to handle than a big, heavy spread that's hard to get on the bed properly.

A comforter, like a duvet, doubles as a bed cover.

Q. The new way of making the bed with layers of stuff has me all mixed up. Does a comforter serve the same purpose as a duvet or do I need both? Is a top sheet used with the duvet now? What kind of decor can this look be used with?

A. Comforter is just another name for a quilt. In colder climates it replaces the duvet. You hardly need both unless the temperature is near zero. Since a bulky comforter is troublesome to wash and dry, a top sheet is needed to keep it clean.

There are arguments for and against the need for top sheets with duvets. Many people prefer to do without a top sheet because it makes tidying up the bed a snap.

On the other hand, duvets unprotected by top sheets get dirty quicker and frequent washings take a toll. Think about it: duvet covers are more expensive to replace than bedsheets.

The look (***illustrated on page 99, bottom right***), using either a comforter or duvet, comes in a wide range of styles and motifs to go with most any kind of decor — especially romantic, country, contemporary, and yuppy casual.❧

MASTER BEDROOMS

Q. What's the easiest way to furnish the master bedroom? I am a new bride, buying furniture for the first time.

A. It's easier, but somewhat less imaginative, to buy in sets. First-time buyers usually go for matching beds or head-boards, night stands, chests, and dressers with mirrors. If space is a problem, they tend to omit the dresser.

As you become more experienced in developing your personal sense of style, you will get the idea of mixing things up to add interest to your bedroom and the rest of your house. Then you can move some pieces out of the original set to other rooms. For example, bedside tables can be shifted to another bedroom and a chest might be used elsewhere to hold linen.

The most important thing to remember, and I shall say this over and over, is to stretch the budget as far as possible to buy the best you can afford. Good furniture will last several lifetimes. If you can buy only one major piece a year, be sure it's a good one. Don't buy junk to make do, thinking that you can upgrade later. Even junk costs money. Instead, get creative. Throughout this book there are ideas on how to use things in different ways — like making ceramic jugs work as tables that can also be used by the bed. Later on the jugs can be moved to a patio or the garden.

Q. We have ordered a contemporary, black-lacquered bedroom set with bone-coloured inlay work. Now we're having second thoughts because the room is small. Should I change the colour to white, which is also available? Or should I mix it up and have a black bed with a white wardrobe and bedside tables? The walls are white.

A. The bedroom set you have already ordered sounds very dramatic. You will loose that drama with a white set because the furniture will blend in with the walls. Also the effect of the bone-coloured inlay work will be lost.

Don't mix it up. The room is too small to have so much going on. Here's what I envision: a black-and-bone colour scheme which is a surprisingly restful combo. Choose a mod bedcover in the same colours and use matching fabric for the window treatment. A black and bone plaid or geometric pattern is just the thing. By the way, soften the walls by painting them bone to coordinate with the colour scheme.

Q. What's the popular look for beds these days? We want something that's in!

A. That's the beauty of New Age Decorating: "Beauty is in the eye of the beholder." Or put another way, "Different strokes for different folks." The trend is towards developing your own personal style instead of doing what everybody else is doing. If your friends are all into buying antique brass beds, that doesn't mean you have to — unless you also crave one. Individuality is the *in* thing.

Having said that, I do believe that looking at what's hot is a good place to start if you don't know what you want. You can decide what's best for you through the process of eliminating the styles you don't like.

Popularity varies from place to place. For example, Niki Lawyer, Director of Inter Design in Bangalore, says that her high-end customers from 30-something-years-old upwards still go for heavily carved beds in teak with a rosewood finish. Not so popular are beds with upholstered headboards. She feels that this is probably true in other Indian metro areas as well.

In some parts of Asia and much of the West, medium-tall four-poster beds are hot items, and Oriental designs with a Chinese flavour are big news. Brass beds are still around and more popular than ever in some places, possibly due to new and diverse styling that makes it an alternative material to wood, which is getting more and more precious.

Check out the current bestsellers at your local retail furniture stores and custom-made furniture shops. Talk to a few in-house decorators[1] for some leads — their advice is usually free.

Q. I fell in love with a brass bed with white trim, but I don't want a cold-looking all-white bedroom. Can I mix brass and wood, or have I made a terrible mistake?

A. Of course you can mix it up as long as the styles are similar. It makes for a more interesting room to get away from so much matchy-matchy.

Dress up your beautiful bed with gorgeous linen to make it the centre of attention. Use warm, earth-coloured patterns with a little white in the background to pull in the wood pieces. Choose a coordinating fabric for the drapes to tie it all together.

Q. We want the master bedroom to be a real show piece. What are the decorating rules for this and how is it done?

A. There are no rules. Your bedroom should be decorated around your own personal whims and quirks. It should be a mirror image of yourself. Therefore feel free to write the script and direct the show. Don't worry about it being a perfect production — pleasing yourself is all that matters.

The main feature of any bedroom is naturally the bed. Give it top billing and dress it first. Since the bed is the biggest thing in the room, decorate it to be the star attraction and make the rest of the room a backdrop for it.

Q. I quite like the idea of using a patchwork quilt for a bedcover to get a cosy country feeling, but I'm wondering if it will look silly here in India. Maybe I should choose something else?

---

1. In-house decorator: a person employed by the furniture store to help customers with their choices. Ask to see a wide range of styles and prices. Remember that they work for the store and many steer potential buyers to high-end items.

A. I don't think you have to worry because there are enough variations of country to go around the world and fit in anywhere. As you can see in the *photo on the opposite page*, it is possible to get a cosy setting using items from all over Asia, including a hand-made patchwork quilt from Thailand.

Patchwork quilts are very popular everywhere because there is a wide selection available in a variety of colours and patterns. For those who aren't looking for cosy, there are quilts that suit even trendy tastes and more sophisticated palates as well. Up-to-date alternatives include quilts that have a dressy Indian motif. They are actually patchworks of old sari pieces.

Q. How many throw pillows do you recommend for decorating a king-sized bed?

A. Any number and a variety of sizes and shapes can be used on any size bed, including a king. It's a matter of preference. Usually an odd number is more interesting than a pair, but it really doesn't matter. Proportion is important though. If you're using just a couple of pillows, they should not be too small for the size for the bed.

The way throw pillows are covered is more significant than the number you use. Do them in colours and patterns that will complement the bedcover and the rest of the room. You can use them to subtly introduce minor accent colours. Above all, make the pillows interesting additions

◄ *Asian "Country"*
This country look is simply a warm and comfortable atmosphere that was created with furniture and accessories from all over Asia — India, Japan, China, Thailand, and Singapore. **Photo by Pallon Daruwala** ❧

to the decor. They should have a reason for being.

Q. I want to put our bed under the window for more air, but then it will face the door and I hate that. The room is small and the ceiling is low. The mattress is on the floor without a frame because I like it that way. Any ideas?

A. It's hard to have it both ways but one solution comes to mind. Create a Cleopatra mood by suspending a canopy of mosquito netting over the mattress and letting it drape on the floor. Cover three sides — head, side and foot, leaving access on the side furthest from the door. What was once a necessity in the tropics is now considered a decorating accessory that adds a great romantic look to the bedroom.

Go ahead and put the bed under the window. The mosquito netting will provide a sense of privacy.

Q. I'd appreciate some ideas on how to give our bedroom a cosy effect without cluttering up the space. It's 4.4 x 2.2 metres (14.5 x 7.5 ft.) with a built-in, wall-to-wall wardrobe. There's only one window located on the short wall at the end of the room.

A. Use colour to get the feeling you want. Paint the walls in a peachy tone, dusty pink, creamy yellow or old ivory for a warm, intimate mood. Do the wardrobe with an oil-based gloss or semi-gloss in the same colour. Don't forget the ceiling. There's no law that says it has to be white. Just use a shade or two lighter than the walls.

Put a cotton durrie[1] on the floor and keep the window dressing simple. I'm thinking of an attractive roller blind to provide privacy, underneath no-fuss cotton tie backs that

---

1. Durrie: a flat-woven Indian rug made of cotton or wool.

end just below the window sill. (*Refer to Chapter 8 for more on window treatments*.) Coordinate or match the curtains to your bed linen in a soft watery pattern with the background colour a shade darker than the walls.

Q. How can I spruce up the master bedroom without spending a lot of money? It has a tired, monotonous look and I need a change.

A. Rearrange the furniture for starters. For something different, don't hesitate to use a well-treated window as a background for the bed. If the room is big enough, angle the bed across a corner to achieve the very latest look.

Switch pictures, wall hangings, lamps and rugs with other rooms. Personalise the master bedroom by surrounding yourself with your favourite things. Group family photographs on the wall, frame postcards and memorabilia from trips for another grouping, and display a personal collection. Add an attractive basket filled with magazines and books for bedtime reading. Drape a shawl over the foot of the bed. (I once draped a hand-crocheted tablecloth across a bed to get an old-fashioned look.) Put out potpourri in clear glass bowls. Place interesting candlesticks on the dresser or night table. Add plants and flowers, even artificial ones are better than nothing. *Voilà!* You've done up a whole new room at practically no expense.

Q. We love our queen-sized bed but it takes up most of the master bedroom. What kind of arrangement and colour scheme will work with the bright yellow built-in wardrobe?

A. Even if there isn't room for large pieces of furniture, you can place a small occasional chair and a little round table with a lamp in a corner. Every bedroom needs a spot for spending some private time.

For more storage and display area, put a combination of cupboards and open shelving over the bed. Either ready-made or built-in units will do. This also eliminates the need for bedside tables. The bright yellow wardrobe isn't a problem. Just paint it to blend in.

To decorate the room, keep it simple. Play down the size of the bed by staying away from busy patterns. Go for a monochromatic or a neutral colour scheme instead. Coordinate the chair cover, bed linen and window treatment for a put-together look.

Q. I'm keen on having a leather headboard, but I've heard that leather starts wearing off after a year or two. Is this true?

A. Not unless the leather is very poor quality and paper thin. Good leather lasts for years and years. However, it may dry out and subsequently crack if exposed to direct sunlight for a prolonged period of time. Therefore it should be rubbed with a product made especially to put the oil back into the leather. Ask your furniture dealer about what to use and how often the leather should be treated to a rub down.

Q. How can I give our bedroom a sophisticated look and still get a cosy feeling? The room has white walls and a tall ceiling that doesn't lend itself to cosy.

A. While many people tend to go for soft, restful hues in the bedroom, sometimes a heavier hand with colour is needed in a room such as you described. Try something like this look that was used in the master bedroom of an old bungalow (*rendering opposite*). The bed was splashed with bold shades of red, blue and green in a bright floral

Flower Power
A bold-patterned fabric in bright colours was the answer for giving some life to a
large, all white bedroom in an old bungalow. The result is warm and cheerful and
inviting — a room you want to spend time in. Rendering by Sheryl Perry 🐦

pattern which dribbles over to the chair in a smaller coordinated design. The traditional brass bed and strong fabrics make for a sophisticated look, while the styling of the gathered bedcover and chair skirting give a friendly, cosy feeling.

To contrast with the white walls, the dark green in the fabric was chosen for an accent colour to use on throw pillows, and some lush green houseplants were added as well. (You can use either real or fake.) In this case the bed was angled and the plants went in the corner behind it.

To personalise your bedroom put familiar things like photographs and your favourite pictures around the room. Potpourri and scented candles are also good for added cosiness.

Q. We want something very different for our master bedroom, and I've found an interesting antique Chinese wedding bed. But we're new to Asia and don't know anything about them. Should I go for it, or is this a crazy idea?

A. (**Photo opposite**) No, it isn't a crazy idea at all. Regional decorating themes are very much in vogue. For some background on the subject, I shall refer you to the following explanation given by my good friend Beverly Cooper. Famous for using exotic, out-of-the-ordinary things to decorate with, Beverly bought an Indonesian-Chinese wedding bed for her master bedroom and had this to say about it:

"Beds like this were made for a bride and groom. Sometimes the groom gave it to the bride as a gift but usually one of the families, probably the groom's, gave it to the couple.

"The newlyweds will spend a certain amount of time

there to get to know each other. It's the only time during their marriage they have the luxury of such privacy. After an undetermined length of time, which varies according to the family, the couple will be moved into other quarters which have one wall and three open sides with just *chik* blinds to pull down in case of rain. Their bed will go with them and, in all likelihood, their babies will be born in that bed."

FYI[1], I have to add that there are often superstitions attached to antique beds because it is likely that over the years somebody has died in them. Many people consider this very bad *karma*[2]. However, if you don't believe in such things, go for it. For what it's worth, Beverly says that they've been sleeping in theirs for several years and nothing bad has ever happened.

Tip: When using a strong regional piece, the rest of the room decor must be in harmony, including additional furnishings, accessories and colours. For example, a Chinese bed does not go with a weak pastel colour scheme surrounded by contemporary furniture.

Q. My husband hates flowers and frills in the bedroom. How can I give our room a more masculine look to please him that will suit me too?

A. Put together a tailored-looking bed ensemble in either stripes, plaids or solids. The **illustration on page 108** shows a sophisticated tailored look that should please both of you. If you prefer a slightly softer look, use a comforter with a box-pleated bed skirt.

Don't over treat the windows. Coordinate the look

---

1. FYI: means for your information.

2. Karma: according to Hinduism and Buddhism beliefs, is destiny determined by one's previous actions.

China Nights
Melinda Alexander's
guest bedroom
houses an exquisite
Indonesian-Chinese
bed, watched over
by a mammoth
Garuda, exactly like
that in Beverly
Cooper's story.
The room is lavishly
decorated with
additional Chinese
furniture and
liberally doused with
red fabrics and
rugs. There's only
one word for
this bedroom —
stunning!
Photo by
Peter Mealin

The simple bed cover is an unfussy look that appeals to both men & women. Keep it light weight, though, for easy handling.

with the bed ensemble and keep it simple with drapes, blinds or Roman shades.

The colour scheme is most important. Don't use sickly pastels. Paint the walls ivory, rich cream or mellow yellow. For the bed and windows use deep blues or dark greens with touches of burgundy.

Q. Our bedroom is so humdrum that it puts me in a bad mood. How can I give it an exciting, fun look?

A. Who could feel bored and out of sorts in a room like interior decorator Rosalie Chidwick's second bedroom shown? She used bold colours and brave prints that are guaranteed to heat things up, using the

adult way to put some fun into a bedroom for grown-ups. The secret is mismatched everything but the basic element is colour.

To copy this look, go through the things you already have for starters. Then work over the sale tables in a big way. Don't worry about things that don't match — that's what you want.

Tip: If a sale pillow cover is too small, jam the pillow down in it, take the end of the pillow cover and give it a twist. Then tie the end up with a ribbon. If the pillow cover is too big, put the pillow in the middle, twist both ends, and tie them off with ribbons.☙

Q. We currently have a very contemporary bedroom, but our tastes are changing. We've taken an interest in antiques. If I switch to an antique bedroom set, can I use our contemporary sheets or do I have to start over?

A. If your sheets aren't wild geometric patterns, you can probably recycle some of them, especially those that are solid colours. Break up the sets and team the existing solids with new traditional prints, stripes or florals.

You can also recycle some checks, plaids and stripes. For example: black and white, electric blue and white, and bright green and white stripes on the bottom team up nicely with a white Battenberg lace top sheet with matching white pillow covers. It's a great look for an antique bed.

Take the old sheets that you're hoping to recycle with you when you go shopping so you can get the colours right.

Q. Can we use a four poster bed in a room with an average 2.5 metre (8-foot) ceiling?

Adults Only
Another one of interior designer Rosalie Chidwick's bedrooms reflects her
preference for using local items to establish a colour scheme and motif.
The effect is interesting and lively. Photo by Rosalie Chidwick

A. Although it's possible, the effect of the tall bed posts are lost with average ceilings. Nothing can take the place of the high ceilings found in older homes to complement the grand looks of a four-poster (**photo opposite**).

On the other hand, a medium-tall four poster like those found on some Indian-styled beds will work quite well in a room with an average ceiling. Look for them in antique shops that also carry reproductions. Choose one to suit your budget — I think this is probably what you need to fit your bedroom (**photo on page 112**).

Q. My husband and I really want a four-poster bed but can't afford it. How can we get the look without buying a new bed?

A. Build a frame that's slightly larger than your bed and attach it to the ceiling. You will place the bed under the frame when the project is completed, so decide where you will want it before you nail up the frame. Attach curtain rods on the inside of the frame at the four corners and hang long curtains that puddle on the floor. The curtains can be made out of any kind of fabric from simple wispy mosquito netting to fancy silk brocade, depending upon the look you want. Put a deep coordinating valance on the outside of the frame. It can be tacked up or attached with velcro.

Q. Our bedroom is big enough to add in some chairs for a

◀ *High Hopes*
The elegance of Melinda Alexander's tall, slim four-poster is accentuated by the high ceiling in her master bedroom. The beautiful accessories are the trademark of Melinda's decorating skills.
Photo by Peter Mealin ❧

seating area, but I don't know how to make it look right. Can you help me?

A. If you have room for two chairs, I recommend using a matching pair. After that, you should keep the chairs within the same style as the rest of the bedroom furniture. They don't have to match the other pieces of furniture; in fact it's better if they don't, but they should be compatible. Create a grouping with one chair on either side of a table of some type. Now you have a nice little area for chatting with a place to set tea or coffee cups. Just add lighting in case you want to do some reading (**photo on page 113**).

Q. Help! Since the recent rainy season, our closets have an awful musty odour that has permeated the clothes as well. What can I do about it?

A. First, empty the closets and wash the interiors with Lysol or Dettol disinfectants to kill any mould that may have got started. Leave the doors open. Next, launder all the washable clothes and hang the rest in the sunshine. If you are lucky enough to own a dryer, you can use it for some things. Put the setting on air-dry or fluff and toss in a fabric-softener sheet or a towel that has been scented with your favourite fragrance.

Only after the closets are thoroughly dried and aired out can you replace everything. Use a fan to hasten drying time. It's a hassle but the only way to get rid of the odour.

Avoid repeats by airing the closets on dryer days, and use the fan again to circulate air and dry out clothes. Also helpful: Damp Rid Dehumidifiers, small plastic containers that contain water-absorbing chemicals. Better solution: if the budget can stand it, room-sized dehumidifiers solve the problem. ❧

Just Right
Robert Mathis's old Indian-styled bed with medium-tall posters suits the average-height ceiling in his flat. Photo by Pallon Daruwala

Compatible Surroundings

This master bedroom includes a pleasant seating area that invites conversation or reading or just plain relaxing. The upholstery of the chairs matches the bed covering and skirting. The table is created out of an old sewing machine base topped with a piece of black granite and covered with white lace to tie in with the other touches of white in the decor. Photo by Pallon Daruwala

BEDROOM MAKE-OVERS

Q. I'm decorating my teenage daughter's bedroom, but I'm looking to the future as well. How can I do up her room now in a young flavour that can also be used later when she graduates without buying all new furniture? The walls are painted peach, and I don't plan to change the colour.

A. I'm going to give you an example of how the same room can be done up to suit your daughter — both now and then — without spending a fortune on new furniture when you have to redecorate. Just buy basic furniture the first time that can be reused in a different way later on. Accessories and decor are the key to success. Here's how:

While the peach walls have predetermined the colour scheme, it's still an easy colour to work with and can liven up the room or soften it, depending on how you play it.

The first setting goes lively and young-looking with a splashy geometric quilt cover and matching pillow case. Since the bed is the biggest thing in the room, the covers are naturally the main attraction. Everything else is chosen to go with it — like a roller blind and computer chair in mottled turquoise and purple tones that blend in perfectly.

Strong turquoise, again picked up from a quilt cover, makes a good accent colour for a bed lamp and halogen desk lamp. Just for fun, a couple of whimsical posters with more touches of turquoise are good propped against the wall. No need to knock more holes.

A noticeboard is the easy and sensible way to hang up favourite pictures and souvenirs that are a part of every teenager's life. Cover it with a black fabric that really looks good against the peach wall. Now you have accomplished a look that any teenage girl would love.

For the next phase in her life, go for a look that reeks of sophistication but still has some touches of little-girl innocence. It's great for college or first-job years. Even

if the budget is tight, you can manage a redo by using what's already there and adding in things as money becomes available.

This time the peach setting goes soft and feminine by changing the bed linen and using more fabrics to dress things up. To get a romantic feeling, trade in the jazzy quilt set for one with a patchwork design. Throw a white crocheted bedspread over the bed. To complete the basic ensemble, cover the window with a white lace curtain and decorated roller blind.

A skirted night table (any kind of table will do) and blue and white accessories will continue the softening-up process. A sheepskin rug is just pure fun to throw casually over the floor. The desk is turned into a make-up vanity and a matching side chair added. Some plants, a new poster and a few of her favourite things placed around to accessorise are the finishing touches.🙶

DOUBLE DUTY

Q. How can we make a small guest bedroom that doubles as a recreation room more interesting? We're bored with the usual bedroomy decor and want something vibrant and colourful.

A. Pick out an unconventional chair, a whimsical lamp and wild little pieces like a funny wall clock. Hang some lively pictures or framed posters. Put up a bulletin board with a collage of amusing snapshots.

To get lively colours, stay close to clean primary shades. In fairly small rooms it's best to use only about two or three different stand-out colours. Small touches of something else are okay. Remember that the room will also be used for sleeping, so you don't want glow-in-the-dark colours and jolting decor.

Q. *To accommodate our large family, our guest room is often used as a second entertaining area. I'm not into sofa beds, so what are my options?*

A. Go for versatile Thai-style futons so you can sleep on them by night and sit on them by day. Best on a raised wooden platform, futons turn a conventional bedroom into a den where friends can chat and lounge around. Dressing up the bed becomes a simple matter of tossing around a few colourful silk pillows (**photo on page 116**).

To complete the den-like feeling, cover the windows with fancy *chiks* that work like Roman shades, which can be raised or lowered according to your needs. Bind the edges in fabric to match the futons for a decorator's touch. To get total privacy, back them up with blackout roller blinds.

Q. *Our young son's room has to double as his bedroom and a playroom for him and his little friends. What's a good theme?*

A. Go for a Disney theme like this example that's suitable for both little boys and preteen girls who aren't yet into the dreamy romantic stage (**rendering on page 117**). The day bed shoved against the wall allows for room to play and gives the kids the grownup feeling of having a sofa in their room.

The cheerful colour scheme is taken from the Mickey Mouse look-alike posters. The bedcover is simply a fitted bottom sheet. If you can't find one in the right colour, or if fitted sheets aren't available in your area, have one sewn up. Be sure the corners are deep enough to fit over the mattress without a struggle. This theme is inexpensive and easy because it's accomplished with colour rather than a lot of accessories.❧

SHARING

Q. *Our two sons will have to share a tiny bedroom. How can we possibly get two of everything in such a small space? Bunk beds are not an option because the ceiling is low.*

A. For a quick lesson on how to handle a small bedroom, study this great example. Furniture placement and simplicity is the key.

Notice the L-shaped arrangement of twin beds that fit snugly into the corners, using up a minimum amount of floor area. You should utilize the space under the beds by having storage drawers for clothing custom-built.

Put in wall-to-wall double shelving mounted high on the wall above the other pieces of furniture, for books and toys to keep the floor free of clutter. With such limited floor space you don't want to be tripping over things.

Even the desk lamps do double duty as work lights

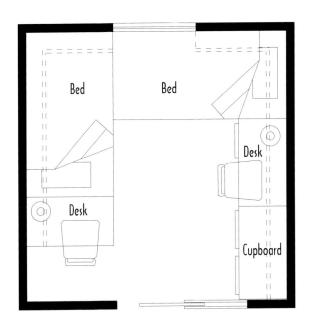

Although tiny, this bedroom can still accommodate the needs of two boys.

Thai Style
An area furnished with Thai-style
futons has flexibility — a place to
relax and chat by day and a place to
sleep by night.
Photo by the author ❧

Just for Kids
This lively theme
is popular for kids
from the toddler
stage to preteens.
It's an inexpensive
look to achieve
and very easy to
change later as the
child grows older.
Rendering by
Sheryl Perry

during study time and reading lights at bedtime. An enclosed cupboard hides the messy items that are better behind closed doors than on the open shelving.

Install a pocket door if possible. If not, replace the normal door with a bi-fold door. This allows for a bit more wall space to hang bulletin boards and decorative posters.

A neutral colour scheme is ideal for a small room and very suitable for boys. Touches of blue and the brightly coloured objects on display keeps the room from looking dull and boring. Use a flat, unobtrusive window treatment like a Roman shade or a decorative roller blind. (*See Chapter 8 for examples.*)

Q. I'm a college girl sharing a small bedroom with my 14-year-old sister who's into the teen scene. We can't agree on anything so how can we decorate the room to suit us both?

A. Since you probably can't agree on furniture either, keep to simple designs. If you want traditional styled twin-beds, buy matching frames and headboards.

On the other hand, if you're ready for something different, your sister can go for a single bed made up in the usual way, and you can go for one that's made up like a daybed with lots of pillows and bolsters.

Additional furniture such as a chest of drawers, desk-cum-dressing table and chairs should match in style and feeling, but different modes will work. For example, you might want a skirted table next to your bed and your sister wants a bedside table with a drawer and shelves. That's not a problem.

However, you must settle on a colour scheme that suits both of you. Something like a black and white combination that goes classic, contemporary, casual, or pop is a great choice. To visually define the your spaces, paint one wall black and three walls white. The teenager gets the black wall because it makes an outstanding background for posters of rock stars and super models.

Then express your personalities with black and white bedcovers in different designs. To accent introduce a third colour from wall hangings for rugs, throw pillows and chair covers. Bright colours such as red, hot pink, sunshine yellow, green, cobalt blue, and rich purple are good. Wishy-washy pastels aren't.

Q. Our son and daughter share a small bedroom. The walls are soft pastel blue, the ceiling and the floor are white. How can I dress up this room to look bigger without getting too feminine or too masculine?

A. To keep the walls from closing in, paint the ceiling blue as well, but go a couple of shades lighter than the walls. This will emphasize the white floor and make the room appear more spacious. Use a simple window treatment that blends in with the walls.

The way the beds are dressed will express your children's individuality. Do one bed in solids and geometric prints or plaids. Do the other one in compatible checks or stripes. It's important to keep the room soft and subtle to conserve visual space. The bed dressings should be in keeping with this feeling. You don't want anything bright or bold that's going to draw your attention to the size of the beds.

Use some white to tie in with the floor. For instance, do a soft yellow and white plaid bedcover for your son with a solid yellow pillow cover and throw pillows in a solid accent colour. Do your daughter's bed in a soft yellow and white stripe, a matching pillow cover or a plaid one that matches your son's bedcover, and white throw pillows. Let the children choose their own ensemble. Whatever their choices, the look will not overpower the small room.

Q. My mother is moving in with us, and we have to give up one of the children's bedrooms. Soon all three kids will have to share one small bedroom. How can I fit in three beds?

A. You don't need three beds. With three children, at least two of them are the same sex and can share a double bed. There is a new version of simple bunk beds, which is the answer to your problem. If you can't find one in the shops, it's an easy design for a furniture maker to copy.

The bottom bunk is a double bed, and the top bunk is a single bed. Put the two who are the same sex on the bottom and the other one on the top. If all three are the same sex, put the two younger on the bottom and the older on the top. ❧

This new idea in bunk beds easily accommodates three kids. The simple design doesn't take up much space.

KIDS' ROOMS

Q. What's new for children's bedrooms? We want a really terrific look that has staying power.

A. The latest kiddy look is really a copy of what yuppy mommies and daddies are going for as seen through the eyes of a child. The tattered Mediterranean theme is big because kids love the bright colours and are more at ease with the uncomplicated decor. It's also easy to keep clean — an added plus.

To make the look suitable for the little ones, use fun fabrics in cool greens and sunny yellows and oranges. Simple curtains and painted furniture, textured walls and the painted floor make for a well-used, comfortable setting. Decorate the walls with the children's handiwork and hang it low enough for them to see.

Q. Where can I get a novelty bed for our son's room? Please give me some ideas for a theme.

A. Many furniture stores also stock kid furniture. Check these out first. If all else fails, you will have to go the custom-made route — easier to do in some places than others. The theme depends on your son's taste and interests. Perhaps he would like a bed in the shape of a racing car or a Batmobile? Does he have a favourite storybook or cartoon character, a hobby or a sport he's really into?

Here's another thought: instead of spending a lot of money on a custom item, why not go for a back-to -nature camping theme? Use a bed frame that resembles a camp cot and form a tent over it with canvas. Give the room a woodsy setting by painting big trees on the walls. It's a look that's easy to change when your son grows out of this stage.

S. Perry '97

Home on the Range

Although this authentic-looking bedroom appears to be straight out of the Wild West, it is actually located in a flat in Southeast Asia. Hunting for accessories to carry out the cowboy theme became a hobby for the Moores and their two sons. Rendering by Sheryl Perry ❧

A Timeless Classic
When Carol Ratcliff
went searching for
antique furniture for
her daughter's new
bedroom, she came up
with an old iron bed.
*"It was love at
first sight,"* Carol says.
*"I recognized the
graceful lines and knew
the bed was just what
I wanted. It cleaned up
beautifully and gives
the room a lighter,
more feminine
feeling than I would
have got with a
wooden bed."*
Rendering by
Sheryl Perry ❧

S. PERRY '97

Simply Comfortable
This user-friendly extra bedroom at Robert Mathis's flat is just the ticket that suits his visiting teenage nephew as well as older guests.
Typical of Robert's unique style, he has reversed the bed, using the taller end that is usually the headboard as the foot of the bed.
Photo by Pallon Daruwala ❧

Q. Our two boys want a cowboy theme for their bedroom. How can I give it a look that will keep them satisfied as they grow up?

A. The best advice I can give on this subject is to relate a real-life experience from my friend Diane Moore (*rendering on page 120*). When their two sons were young, Diane decided on bunk beds for them which inspired her to help them decide on a Western cowboy theme. She said that the idea seemed to suit the boys at the time, and over the years one thing led to another.

Although the room looks authentic, it's actually located in an apartment in southeast Asia and the decorations came from all parts of the world. For example, the wood chair is from South Africa. The boys thought it looked like it came from an old-time American saloon, so Diane went a step further by adding in the antique solid brass spittoon. "That was Paul's acquisition," Diane says referring to her husband. "It's a special piece that he picked up for 25 cents (Rs 12) at his first antique auction and was what started us off on our lifetime quest for interesting antiques."

The antique schoolhouse brass bell, placed on the bookcase, also came from an auction, and the old wall clock was bought in an antique shop in Malaysia more than 30 years ago. The bed quilts are family heirlooms. One was made by the boys' great-grandmother, and the other one was hand sewn by their great-great-grandmother.

Not everything in the room is old though, and ready access to look-alike decorations makes the cowboy theme easy to duplicate. I think your idea is wonderful. Hunting for things to add to the room can become a hobby that will involve your sons and the whole family.

Q. Please give me an inspiration for decorating our daughter's bedroom. She's the dreamy type who loves to read.

A. Give her a perfect story-book setting with puffy white curtains and a layered white linen and Battenberg lace bed ensemble (*photo on page 94*). Pile the bed with throw pillows and include some stuffed toys around the room.

Be sure to provide a bedside lamp that is good for reading. The lamp in the illustration is a good example because it's high enough for both the bed and nearby chair.

The basically white colour scheme works without being boring when it's accessorised right. The look and feeling of this room is endearing and lasting. Your daughter will love it!

Q. My mother gave us an old iron bed for our daughter's room. I don't want to hurt her feelings, but I don't know what to do with it because the finish is a mess.

A. Most likely the bed frame is covered with several layers of ancient paint mingled with rust and gunk, so you need to have the finish completely stripped off. When you finally get down to the original iron work, it should be sanded down with a fine grade of sandpaper. Then the frame should be painted with an anti-rust preparation before new paint is applied. In the *rendering on page 121,* you can see a good example of a lovely antique iron bed that was refurbished and painted white.

Q. Our son has gone off to university, and I want to redo his room. What is suitable for his infrequent visits?

A. Use a simple, uncluttered look that will be comfortable for him and, at the same time, allow you to turn it into a guest room when he's away. Space is too precious to sit idle. Something like the bedroom pictured *opposite* will be just the thing to serve both purposes.

CHAPTER 6

Gathering Places

INTRODUCTION

The ways we use space change as our needs change. At one point of family life, a spare room may be used for a play area for the little ones. Later it can become a study room for teenagers and a place to hang out while they can listen to CDs with their friends. Still later that same room can be the quiet spot where Mom and Dad relax, watch TV or read. After all, a room is only four walls. What we chose to do in that room is up to us and our prevailing requirements.

Certainly, as the activities shift the decor of this room must also be varied for that is often what defines its purpose. The only thing to remember is that the setting should be user-friendly and attractively decorated.

All too often, though, we just don't have the luxury of having that spare room. Usually this happens when the children are growing up, every room is occupied, and the house is bursting at the seams. It is times like these when we most need a little extra space. One of the ways to expand your house is to incorporate outside areas and treat them as additional rooms without walls. A patio can become an open-air family room, a balcony can be a cosy conversation area, and a garden can be — well, almost anything you want it to be (*illustration on page 126*).

Outdoor Living
Lush tropical plants and
the soothing sound of
trickling water draws
everyone to the coolness
of this garden —
the perfect spot for an
open-air gathering place.
Rendering by
Sheryl Perry

Q. *We have an unusual ceiling in our family room. It's high and angular. We'd like to do something interesting. Any ideas?*

A. I shall refer to another example done by the talented Joan Griffes (**pictured on page 128**). In their casual family/TV room, she painted part of the ceiling an accent colour to emphasize the architectural features of the room. Not only did this successfully bring out the lines and interesting angles of the ceiling, the paint Joan chose set the tone for her entire colour scheme. This isn't surprising because everything in the room is perfectly coordinated, including the needlepoint wall hanging from Nepal and the two Chinese vases.

Joan's special decorating touch is practical as well as unique. For example, the sofa is actually a twin bed so the room can do double duty as a guest room when needed. The round, skirted table is really a small, unused dryer fitted with a piece of round plywood on top. Not pictured is her TV; this is placed on a large base covered in the same black and white plaid as the sofa. The base is the large, sturdy box the TV came in, which they saved to ship the TV in the next time they move. What lovely ideas for ways to use these things we don't know what to do with — especially when there's a shortage of storage space.

Q. *We are building a new house and are wondering about the sizes of the living room and the family room. Should we have a small living room that's more of a sitting room and a large family room for entertaining or vice versa?*

A. The ideal is to have a floor plan that lends itself to swapping. For example, if you have young children, you may want a large living room for entertaining your friends and relatives, and a smaller family room so the kids can watch TV and videos without disturbing you. Later on when the kids get old enough to have their own friends over, the smaller room can become the living room for adult conversations, and the larger room becomes the family room for young people's parties. Eventually after the kids leave home, Mom and Dad can once again take over the larger room for entertaining, and the smaller room becomes their personal space in the form of a study or a TV room.

Q. *We bought some lovely leather furniture for the TV room, and the existing ruffled tie-back sheers don't seem right anymore. Should we change them?*

A. Yes, I'm afraid so. Leather furniture and sheer, ruffled curtains are not soulmates. The result is a ridiculously un-balanced mixture. Match bold trendy window treatments with modern leather furniture and use stately-but-new looks with traditionally-styled leather furniture. Rule of thumb: window treatments and furniture should have the same feeling and weight.

Q. *We're building a new house with a small family room and want it to be something special. What do you advise?*

A. If it's a totally unique look that you're after, how about an *avant-garde* approach that includes building in the furniture and literally making it part of the room. This technique moulds the furnishings right into the walls, which is also a great space-saving device. The style sets the theme and there are several which are especially suitable namely ultra modern, rustic and Mediterranean. For Simran Gupta's version, which she calls Mexican, see the **photo on page 129.**

High Colour
Joan Griffes highlighted the unusual architectural features of the ceiling by painting the angular beams in soft turquoise, which sets the colour scheme for the room. Photo by Pallon Daruwala ❧

Built-in Style

A new way to furnish a room is to literally build everything into the room like Simran Gupta did in her home. She chose a Mexican theme supported by dramatic walls, special-effects lighting, and carefully placed accessories. Photo by Pallon Daruwala ❧

Q. We need a coffee table for our great room, but there's a problem. Our present seating arrangement requires a large table to fill up space, but soon we will be moving to another home that has a small living hall and a spare room that we will use as a study-cum-TV room. What kind of table would suit both places?

A. You are wise to be thinking ahead. With prices soaring out of sight, we can no longer afford to pitch out perfectly good things. Recycling has become a way of life. To accommodate today's conservative market, furniture makers are designing more flexible pieces that are meant to be moved around and used in different ways. For example, four small square tables placed close together can function as one large square coffee table. On the other hand, the tables can be separated for any number of possibilities.

In another situation, you could make a narrow rectangular arrangement using two or three tables in a row. The left-over table(s) can go at the end of the sofa or a chair. Add a tall substantial lamp and you have a new side table.

Simple styles will work with almost any kind of decor which also allows you to move them from room to room. They can even be switched to a bedroom where they would make good-looking bedside tables.

Q. We have a low rosewood coffee table (61 x 152 cms/ 2 x 5 ft.) in our family room and don't know how to place it.

A. Create a comfortable seating area around your big coffee table that says to your guests, "Hey! Come and sit here." Put a three-seater sofa on one side, balanced by a two-seater sofa or two chairs opposite. If the room is narrow, place a chair at each end of the coffee table instead of opposite the three-seater.

Q. We'd like to continue using our dark brown rattan sofa set in the family room, but part of the paint has come off. Can you tell us how to redo it in the same dark colour, which we prefer, without spending too much on it.

A. Rattan takes to spray paint very well. It's easy to do and you can save money by spraying it yourself. Enamel auto spray paint should work. Just follow the simple instructions on the can. If you repaint it the same colour, one coat may be enough to make the set look like new. However, if the set has been varnished, you need to paint it with a primer first to give the paint a base.

Q. I can't find a TV cabinet I like. Where can I find something with a unique or distinctive design in natural wood? Good quality is a must and the budget is flexible.

A. You may want to have a cabinet custom built. Some cabinetmakers will design one for you, and some can copy a design of your choice. Either way, you should have a few ideas when you call on these people so read all the decorating magazines you can. Tear out pictures of your favourite TV cabinets and/or entertainment centres, and develop a file folder. Review it about every week, tossing out the pictures that no longer appeal to you. This weeding-out process can prevent expensive mistakes.

Alternatively, you should consider converting a beautiful piece of furniture like an armoire, a sideboard, or an antique chest into a TV cabinet.

Q. I work out of my home and recently converted a guest bedroom into a study. Now I have a houseguest coming for an extended visit. I know a sofa bed is the answer for sleeping arrangement, but she will not have much privacy because I have to work in the same room. What should I do?

A. Yes, you need to have a sofa bed[1] in your study. But instead of installing your guest in the study, why not give her your bedroom and you can take over the sofa bed. That way, you can work without stressing over whether or not you are getting your guest out of bed too early in the mornings or keeping her up too late at night.

Q. How should my home office be organised for the best efficiency?

A. The first thing that comes to mind is that everything should be within easy reach so you don't have to keep jumping up and down. Not only is that obviously a waste of time, it also breaks your concentration. You need to have a telephone on your desk. If the budget can't handle an extension, get a cordless model that you can take to your desk when you are working. Reference books should be kept handy and arranged in a way that makes sense. Files should be in a convenient location — either a deep desk drawer or a small two-drawer filing cabinet is usually adequate. And the one thing I can't work without, a chair on rollers that lets me scoot over to get something I can't quite reach and back again to my desk. Of course, the chair must be adjustable so the desk is the right height to avoid hand and wrist problems. Try out a few positions to see what is comfortable, but it is usually best to keep your arms close to your sides with elbows and wrists fairly level and feeling relaxed.

Give yourself plenty of surface space for writing and working, which is getting harder to do with all the office equipment we have these days. Clean everything off your desk that is not necessary to your current task, including personal items like framed pictures. Get into the habit of putting things like files and books back in their proper place when you have finished with them.

If your writing surface is not smooth, cover it with a piece of clear glass. This also gives you an excellent place to display those favourite photos and things like phone lists and a small, yearly calendar. Be sure to use spacers between the surface top and the glass so it won't stick to items and ruin them[2].

An orderly desk makes for better work habits. Arrange things so they're easy to get to by placing the telephone on your left side if you're right-handed or vice versa if you're left-handed to free your writing arm to take down notes. Keep pencils, pens and erasers in a separate container from other tools of the trade like brushes, markers and scissors — attractive coffee mugs work just as well as expensive pencil holders.

Don't jumble up your desk drawers. You save valuable time when you don't have to dig around for things. Use the main drawer — usually the shallow one across the front — for keeping frequently used items like paper clips, stamps, a stapler, and your diary. Keep fresh paper supplies in a separate drawer.

Keep your tasks prioritised with labelled file folders such as one for projects that require your immediate attention, one for things that can be put off for now, and one for information that you might use later. And lastly, here is a habit I formed many years ago: clean off your desk

---

1. The trendy name for sofa beds is convertible sofas.
2. As I have mentioned in other chapters, spacers are necessary when glass, marble, granite, and other materials are placed on top of wood surfaces.

when you shut down for the night. There is something very inviting about a tidy work space.

Q. How can I decorate a small, oddly shaped room that we want to use for a study/TV room?

A. Avoid the fluff and take a simple approach. Robert Mathis set a good example in the study of his flat where even the wall hangings are kept to a minimum with a single handsome painting. The absence of tables allows enough room for a full-sized leather sofa, a matching arm chair, and a small, roll-top writing desk. On the wall opposite the desk, there is enough room for a TV set. The mood is established with colour and the no-nonsense furnishings — very effective and tempting, a room that you want to be in (**photo opposite**).

Q. What can we do about the small bedrooms our two little boys have? There is no room for them to play and nowhere to store their toys.

A. For now, I suggest doubling up the boys in one bedroom. Bunk beds are the best space savers. The extra bedroom you now have to work with can become their playroom. If the new playroom is next to or close to their bedroom, paint the walls a similar colour and keep the decor synchronised for continuity.

Divide the play room into two equal parts. Each part should contain a toy box with a substantial lid so it can serve as a table for colouring or painting pictures and playing games. Add shelving to stash additional toys, books and games. Keep everything within reach. You can add more shelves as the boys grow. Kids will invariably climb on shelves that go up too high and that is dangerous. Not only can the

little ones fall and hurt themselves, the shelves can be ripped out of the walls and come crashing down, kids and all. Free-standing shelves have a tendency to topple over.

To make the room appear bigger, paint the shelving to match the walls. Decorate the walls above the shelves with posters that suit the interests of each boy. This further defines their personal space. Low furnishings for the convenience of little people will make the room bottom heavy. Therefore to balance out things, run the posters and other wall decorations up the walls. Put up a wall-paper border, paint or stencil on a design a couple of inches below the ceiling for a finishing touch.

Setting aside a separate room for a play area is a practical solution for space problems because you are confining a perpetually messy situation to one room. A bedroom that is only used for sleeping is not so hard to keep tidy. This way, when company comes, you can simply close the play-room door to hide the clutter.

Q. Where can I find a place to call my own away from the bustle and noise of the living room?

A. Look around your home for an unused corner, the end of a corridor, or a short wall that isn't being utilised. Even in the most chock-a-block homes, you can usually find a tiny space to make into your own private spot.

For example, the **rendering on page 134** shows a previously bland corner that was transformed into a quiet reading lair for this homeowner. The area is actually a very small space just outside the loo. Since it isn't big enough for an arm chair, an extra dining room chair works just fine. The chest and accessories were borrowed from other rooms. By placing the small lamp next to a mirror, the amount of light is doubled, thus making the corner bright enough for reading.

Compact Drama
A rich, monochromatic colour scheme works wonders in Robert Mathis's study to soften
the sharp angles and to make the room appear larger. Photo by Pallon Daruwala

Reading Corner
Even the tiniest corner
can be set up to make
an attractive quiet
place. This one is lighted
for easy reading.
Rendering
by Sheryl Perry

Room Addition
Gill Hough added space to her flat by transforming an ordinary, rather
unappealing balcony into a cosy open-air sitting room.
Photo by Pallon Daruwala

Hanging Garden
Balconies are ideal for
growing plants, which
can be grouped from top
to bottom in even the
most limiting space.
Rendering
by Sheryl Perry ❧

Eye Appealing
*Stone patios need a spot of greenery for interest. This home owner built an eye-catching
mini garden and made it low maintenance too. The rock bed keeps weeds to a minimum.*
Rendering by Sheryl Perry ❧

Q. How can I make a tiny, unattractive balcony more inviting? There is nothing special about it and it doesn't have a view.

A. When Gill Hough faced the same dilemma at her flat, she saw an opportunity to try her hand at creative decorating. Nature's own colour palette of green, terracotta and white give the balcony a refreshing, airy feeling that is pleasant to look at from the inside as well. After the walls were given a fresh coat of white paint, vines and tall topiaries in terracotta pots were applied using both stencils and handpainted techniques. An ugly brick wall that faced the balcony was screened from sight by ordinary *chiks* and real yellow palms planted in terracotta clay pots to match the floor tiles and stencil designs. The result is a cosy seating area for two with a handpainted view (***photo on page 135***).

Tip: A small balcony makes a handy bar area for parties. All you have to do is equip it with an ice chest for cold drinks, a table for serving them and a bartender.

Q. I have a utility balcony off the kitchen that I use for growing plants. I'd like to make better use of the space but can't give up my tiny garden area. Any suggestions?

A. It's not impossible to "have your cake and eat it too," in this case. The location of your balcony off the kitchen makes it a natural place for alfresco dining. Even the smallest space can take a little round table. Use side chairs without arms that tuck up under the table. Suspend your plants from the ceiling and place them along the top of the wall and in the corners. Add a ceiling fan, if possible, to stir the air on sultry days and to help keep the mosquitoes at bay. See the ***illustration on page 136.***

Q. Our patio is very ordinary. What can we do to dress it up?

A. Create an unusual focal point to make your patio more inviting. I suggest a small, easycare garden like the one ***illustrated on page 137.*** To give it an interesting shape, have a semi-circle or oval cut out of the surface at the edge of the patio. The rock base for the garden serves a two-fold purpose: it discourages the growth of weeds, which makes the garden more manageable, and it gives a visual continuity to the hard surface of the patio.

Q. Our garden is in sad shape. We've lost a royal palm, a mango tree is dying, and other plants are in trouble. Can you recommend someone to tell us what's happening?

A. Get to the root of your problems — get an expert from a major nursery to diagnose diseases and viruses, determine the presence of parasites and bugs, check for nutrient deficiencies in the soil, and recommend proper treatment. The service may not be free so be sure to ask about charges.

Tip: To be safe, always consult your gardener about fertilizer — and insecticide as well. Too little won't be effective, too much will kill your plants, and the wrong kind can do either.

Q. What kind of plants can I grow on our balcony? It only gets the morning sun.

A. Your growing area sounds like the perfect place for more sensitive potted plants that can handle only partial sun, which means not more than half a day. **Hydrangea, money**

*Clockwise from 12 o'clock:
Croton, Bougainvillaea, Plumbago,
Adenium, Allamanda, and (centre)
Polyscias.* Photo by author ❧

*Clockwise from 12 o'clock:
Cordyline, Cactus, Yucca, and Song
of India.* Photo by author ❧

Wall Flowers
Visitors to May Kottukapally-Demann's garden are treated to gobs of colour that runs from
her carefully selected plants right up the wall, which is the palette for cheerful, tribal art.
Photo by author ❧

plant, **yellow palm**, and some types of **ferns** should work for you. Hydrangea even does well on shady, but not dark, balconies and also can be enjoyed inside for one or two months after it's in bloom.

Q. I want some flowering plants in our garden, but everything burns up. Any suggestions?

A. Perhaps you aren't putting in the right kind of plants. You need things that can take the heat like the ever popular and versatile **Bougainvillaea**. It is happiest when drenched in hot sun and flowers profusely in a variety of colours. **Allamanda**, also known as Golden Trumpet, is a bush with waxy yellow flowers that loves warm sunshine. It does equally well in the ground or potted. **Plumbago** is a small shrub and quite good for sunny window boxes as well as pots. Little blue flowers bloom constantly since this plant has no season. **Pachystachys**, also called Lollipops, and **Shrimp Plants** thrive in the same kind of environment. Just keep cutting them back to make them bushy. Be sure to consider **Balsam** for window boxes also. The plants are rather scrubby looking, but the bright crimson flowers are worthwhile. It's one of the best and most economical choices because the seeds drop off and germinate again by themselves. Balsam grows prolifically in our garden in both full and partial sun, sometimes sprouting up in the most unlikely places when the wind blows the seeds about. However, this isn't a problem for window-box gardeners.

Adenium or Desert Rose is a very hardy flowering plant, especially suitable for pots in tight places like balconies that don't get a lot of circulating air or much night-time dew.

Although Adenium certainly is a locally common sun lover, beware! Like many other plants, it can be highly poisonous. You should always ask a professional about those you buy, especially if you have small children around or pets that chew on things.

When you have no time to fiddle but still crave flowering greenery, a potted slow-growing **Euphorbia**, better known as Crown-of-Thorns, is just the thing. Needing very little water and only occasional pruning, it's almost maintenance free.

If you decide to try your hand at growing some non-flowering leafy plants that can be potted for full or even partial sun, **Polyscias, Crotons and Cordyline** are good. Crotons are very decorative with leaves ranging from yellow to green to red and spotted versions as well. Cordyline changes colour according to the percentage of sun exposure. **Song of India, Yucca and Cactus** are happy in either full or partial sun (*photos on page 139*).

Q. Do you have an idea how we can accessorise our garden with something besides the run-of-the-mill statuary?

A. I recommend that you consider a truly unique way to decorate your garden, which makes statuary altogether unnecessary — paint the walls with amusing pictures instead of setting things around. A good example is found at the home of May Kottukapally-Demann. Her passion for tribal art was the impetus for her very special garden decor — a gaily painted wall in the brightest colours with cheerful figures that are guaranteed to bring smiles to all of her guests who gather there (*photo opposite*).

CHAPTER 7

Bathrooms
& Loos

INTRODUCTION

Attitudes are drastically changing towards the little room that houses the facilities. And it can't change fast enough to suit me. There is no reason for a bathroom to be barely more than an outhouse moved indoors — space is too precious to waste. Today's bathroom must be more than functional.

Decorators, architects and trendsetters are turning the bathroom into a private comfort zone and loading it with all the amenities necessary for personal pampering. It's a place to relax and escape from the daily grind in total seclusion — the ultimate refuge. The modern bathroom reflects one's lifestyle and personal taste and is decked out with the latest state-of-the-art technology in a high-fashion setting. And the public is going for this revolutionary concept in a big way.

In response to the clamour for glamour, gadgets and convenience, architects are allowing more space for bigger bathrooms. And people are spending more for the pure pleasure of pampering themselves. If they can't build something new, they are upgrading their existing bathrooms.

At high-end markets customers are demanding more luxury items, paying more attention to the look of accessories like towel racks, mirrors, even paperholders and soapdishes, and are definitely fashion-oriented. These creature comforts have a princely price tag. Outfitting a fully equipped lux bathroom, either new or remodelled, runs from Rs 2.5 lakhs upwards plus contractor and installation fees!

At the other end of the pole are budget-conscious young couples who go for the basics in a contemporary motif. They can expect to pay far less to outfit a small bathroom (3.25 sq. metres/35 sq. ft.) with the bare essentials — tub, tiles and lighting. A mid-range

Dressed for Guests
While the architectural details
of this guest loo provide much
of the decorations, gobs of
accessories were added
to dress it to the hilt.
Photo by Pallon Daruwala ⚓

bathroom that includes the essentials with a few lux items thrown in (but, very few) will cost Rs 40,000 to Rs 50,000 upwards.

European trends are the local rage: matching wall tiles and fixtures, faucets that don't look like faucets, matte-finished fixtures and recessed shelving. Double basins either free-standing or set in a vanity are preferred. Vogue decor is achieved by laying plain tiles in colour patterns and combinations. Track lighting and recessed spots are *in*. (The local standard still calls for fluorescent lighting, but please use warm-white tubes.)

Big is *in* and multi-roomed bath suites are news. Separate areas are earmarked for dressing and making-up, wardrobes, tub and shower, commode and bidet, and even exercise equipment.

Bidets are *in* but slow to catch on here. While the upmarket customers are installing them, I wonder how many are actually using them.

Bath tubs are certainly *in*. Although people generally aren't about to give up their beloved showers for quick daily use, they are adding tubs in the main baths. No comfort zone is complete without a tub — even a spa — for leisurely, weekend soaks when one has more time. Another reason to splurge on a tub is to give the kids a place to splash and cool off on hot summer days. However, a shower is necessary too.

Marble and granite are the *in* alternatives to wall tiles. But one should forego the tempting wallpapers and borders, which won't stand up in this climate.

Glass blocks are the latest *in* look. Locally they are pricey, so plan to use them sparingly, as partitions between tub and commode for example.

STARTING FRESH

Q. How can we outfit the bathroom in our new house for the convenience of those who will be using it? We also need some decorating ideas.

A. When several people are using the same bathroom, a set of twin sinks comes in handy. That way, at least two people can be attending to their morning rituals at the same time. May Kottukapally-Demann, my friend whom you met in previous chapters, had just this in mind when she planned her new home. To save space, she chose twin pedestal sinks placed close together instead of vanities. The wall above was fitted with cabinets for storage. And here's where May's unique sense of decorating comes into play.

To carry out the tribal theme of her home, the cabinet doors are Rajasthani with mirrors inset. She hired Gujarati artists to paint tribal figures and designs on the walls. Even the light switch is camouflaged with designs (**photo on page 146**).

Q. We are saving up for our dream home and want to plan ahead. What are the trends in bathroom fashions?

A. Watch for architectural styling that make the bathroom fit the rest of the house — like a pitched ceiling to go with contemporary, fake beams for European country, and pillars for neoclassic.

Recessed "can" lights in the ceiling will go with a dimmer switch for those times when you don't need the brights on.

Windows will get a clean treatment with mini blinds and plantation shutters that are practical and up-to-the-mark in looks.

Old fashioned brass taps with lever-like handles and shower head and fixings to match are big and getting bigger. Ceramic set-in soapdishes and toilet paper holders are out and considered tacky.

You'll see stately pedestal sinks replacing built-ins, but it's interesting to mix it up when you have more than one

Room for Two
To speed up morning rituals, May Kottukapally-Demann
installed twin pedestal sinks in the all-purpose bathroom of
her Bangalore home. The tribal theme of the house is
faithfully carried out in the brightly coloured, handpainted
wall designs and accessories.
Photo by Pallon Daruwala ❧

bathroom.

Furnished bathrooms will gain in popularity. A chest provides storage when you go for pedestal sinks, and an Oriental rug in the powder room is unquestionably elegant.

Always look for ways to add your personal touch — that extra something that says, "This room is part of my house too."

Q. What colours do you suggest for our new bathroom?

A. The chequered past of black and white is back in, but with the fresh look of bold, bright red accessories. Walls are white tile with black tile trimming. Fixtures are white or black. Red faucets, taps, shower heads, hooks, towel racks, soapdishes, towels, and accessories complete the look.

Also *in* are matching tiles and fixtures in the softest colours, much more delicate than the pinks, blues, greens and yellows of yesterday; velvety dove-grey, barely beige, bisque, and classic white.

While almost anything goes these days, sickly-sweet pastels and drab dreary colours like maroon, dark brown, harvest gold, avocado green, and overpowering colours such as autumn orange are not popular. However, if some of these colours are your favourites, don't despair. Many of them are reappearing in more muted shades.

Q. What is the current trend in bathroom fixings?

A. Stylish sanitaryware is *in*. Fashion favourites range from elegant neo-classic (yes, even in bathrooms) to shiny hi-tech with popular in-between choices of old-world Edwardian, romantic Victorian, art deco, and post-WWII styling. Pedestal basins and wall-hung commodes are the newest contemporary look. The main idea is to pick a period theme and carry it out with coordinated wall and floor tiles, towels and accessories.

Tastefully done, designer bathrooms are *in*. The last word in elegance includes gold- and silver-plated basins, gold swans that spew water, chrome waterfall faucets, and basins set in antique furniture.

Do avoid very trendy colours though. They not only date your bathroom, it becomes difficult to find co-ordinated towels and accessories when the colours go out of fashion.

Q. We want a hi-tech look for our new bathroom we won't get tired of or won't go out of style. Any suggestions on how to do this?

A. Choose good quality, traditional fixtures in white. Don't be tempted by trendy designs and colours that might date your bathroom in a few years.

Clever new home owners are going for classic tiling and setting the style with accessories. Black and white tiling with shiny chrome or lipstick red drawer pulls, towel racks, toilet paper and toothbrush holders, and soapdishes work for a hi-tech look.

When your tastes change, put up new towel racks and accessories that define a different style.

Q. Is there anything new in bathroom tiles? The usual is so ho-hum, but I can't go all out on some fad either.

A. Go for classic — the style has been around for centuries. Get the look by laying tiles in geometric patterns. Ceramic tiles of black, beige and white, or dark green and white are great colour combinations (*illustration on this page*).

The newest way to get that old feeling is with mosaic tiles. A look that has been around forever and was especially popular in the 1950s is available now in 25 mm squares (1 sq. in) of ceramic, marble and stone. Go all the

Classic 25 mm (1 in.) black and white chequer-board tiles are always popular.

way, using them for the entire floor or for borders. Or, put down a permanent "throw rug" with a mosaic design laid in the middle of the floor for a swanky look.

If the pocketbook can't stand that kind of pressure, substitute a border tile in printed mosaic patterns available at most tile shops. Be on the lookout for old squares of mosaic tile designs at give-away prices.

Tip: Although mosaic tiles are also available in glass, these are most often used on walls and counter tops. Check with a tile expert before using them on the floor.

Q. Are locally made tiles recommended for bathroom floors?

A. Porous, locally made tiles should be avoided whenever possible because they are not completely anti-slip, are easily stained, and are difficult to coordinate with ceramic wall tiles. Now ceramic floor tiles with an anti-slip surface are available.

Vinyl tiles (aka rubber tiles) are not being used — except in bottom-of-the-line, budget bathrooms. They just aren't smart in this climate because moisture makes the glue lift up.

Q. What's best to use for grouting? I thought rubberised stripping was the thing, but now I hear it isn't very good.

A. Cement is the best grouting and sealing material. Although it cracks in time, it's easily repaired by adding more cement. Silicon is a good sealer, but it's susceptible to fungus that won't come off. When it gets unbearably yukky, silicon must be stripped off completely and newly applied. A fungus resistant silicon may soon be available.

The experts don't recommend rubberised stripping because it isn't a lasting solution. It tends to shrink and peel.

Q. We want the new bathroom our children will be using to look youthful but not something they will outgrow. Do you have some suggestions?

A. A blue and white colour scheme is very flexible and works for all age groups. The blue must be strong to contrast with white — not pale or pastel. When the kids are little, a nursery rhyme theme with primary colours for accents is great. As they grow up, the themes can change while the blue and white background remains the same.

Do the walls in practical white tiles and add a blue border. The floor can be done with matching blue tiles. If you have any wall space showing that isn't tiled, paint it to match the blue border and flooring. Paint the ceiling light sky blue and then paint on fluffy white clouds. You and the kids will love it! (***See photo on page 207.***)

When you want to change the theme, just repaint the walls and ceiling. Most robust colours like sunshine yellow, bright green or raspberry will look great with blue and white.

Q. We plan to sell our home in about five years time. What kind of popular bathroom gadgets can we install in the meantime that will appeal to prospective buyers?

A. You are so smart to look ahead. In most cases, bathroom and kitchen improvements are good investments, and you will get your money back when you sell or rent. The best thing about adding gadgetry is that it can be installed as the pocketbook allows, so you won't have big outlays of cash all at one time.

Everything goes in the bathroom now for the sake of convenience. Wall-mounted hair driers and magnifying mirrors are hotel ideas copied for home use. Lighted make-up mirrors are hot items. Massaging shower heads and multiple, pulsating shower jets are popular. (Be sure you have enough water pressure before you run out to buy one of these.) Piped-in music, telephones and bar refrigerators haven't caught on yet, but don't be surprised when they do! ❧

Re-dos

Q. The master bedroom of our terrace home has no en suite bath, but there's room to add one. How much will it cost for average quality everything? Oh, there aren't any water pipes or sewage drains around that area.

A. You should allow at least Rs 50,000 for the necessities like tub, commode, sink, lighting, and tiling. Installation and labour are extra. I have no idea what it will cost to add on a bathroom, but it won't be cheap. Additional plumbing is an expensive proposition. You need a bathroom specialist to do the planning and a minimum of three reliable contractors to provide accurate estimates. They can also advise you about building regulations. Add 10%–15% onto the estimate you go with to cover unforeseen expenses.

Q. We're renovating our home and want to add a bathroom off the master bedroom. We need a guest bath too, but don't have the space for both. Any ideas?

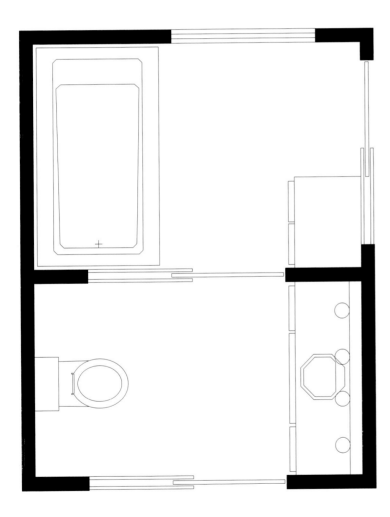

Two entries make this split bathroom accessible to both the guest area and the master bedroom. ❧

A. No problem. Just arrange things for two entries into the bathroom — one from the bedroom and one from the public areas.

If possible, place the fixtures so you can divide the space to hide the tub area from company. Dress up the guest bathroom portion that holds the sink and commode with handsome accessories. Since that part of the room will also be used as your private bathroom, add convenience features like make-up lights for you and a wall-mounted shaving mirror for him. Include a dimmer switch so the lighting can be adjusted to suit the mood for your guests.

The floor plan on the left shows how Susheela Vishvanathan made her bathroom do double duty by splitting it into two important areas. The 1.5 x 1.8 metres (5 x 6 ft.) bathing area that is adjacent to their bedroom holds a tub/shower combination and a chest of drawers for extra storage. Susheela hung a lovely, framed mirror over the chest because, as she says, "A bathroom just can't have too many mirrors."

The other section of the bathroom is accessible from the public areas and used by the guests as well as by the residents. The space is just 1.2 x 1.8 metres (4 x 6 ft.), but it is large enough to hold a long vanity with plenty of room for storing supplies and toiletries. The entire wall above the vanity is mirrored.

Q. How can I add storage space when we redo our small bathroom? We have a limited budget.

A. There are inexpensive ways to add places to stash things even in the smallest bathroom. Plan ahead for built-in shelves that recess into the walls — a great space-saver. Place attractive shelving for toiletries in otherwise wasted areas — over the basin and commode, and in shower and tub corners. Buy shower and tub caddies. Install the basin in a vanity for stowing necessities. Store extra towels in baskets. Pick up extra cupboard space by hanging wire racks on the inside of the doors. Organise shelf space with storage bins to hold makeup and toiletries.

Space and money are precious commodities. Consult the experts to get the most out of both. Designers specialising in bathroom interiors at upscale bathroom shops will help you plan your renovations. Their services are usually free. They will advise you on sanitaryware placement and can recommend contractors. They will also tell you how far you can stretch your budget. How, you say? Simple. They help you choose themes for each bathroom and achieve the desired effect with bold and imaginative accessories.

Q. Is it a good idea to install sliding-glass doors on our bathtub?

A. Personally, I find them a pain to keep clean because the tracks for the sliding doors collect moisture, dirt, mildew, and grunge. Very often they have to be scrubbed out with a toothbrush.

With a little creativity, shower curtains can be done up very attractively. The tub can be draped with fabric panels either hanging straight or tied back on each side. You can do it plain or fancy up the treatment with a valance, fringe and tassels. On a separate rod hang a clear plastic or solid-coloured shower curtain that coordinates with the fabric. Another advantage to shower curtains is they're easy to change around for new looks when you get tired of the old way.❧

MAKE-OVERS

Q. We want to give our old bathroom a more fashionable look. What can we do without replacing everything?

A. The easiest way to update a tired-looking bathroom is to paint it. If the whole room is tiled, paint the ceiling, cabinetry, door, and framework. Don't be afraid of using colour. Change out the accessories and drawer pulls to fit in with a theme like the sea creatures *illustrated below.* There are some very clever designs available that will add lots of appeal at very little expense.

Work on giving the floor a spectacular new look. Go for Italian mosaic tiles, an ancient art form that originated in Mesopotamia from Islamic designs. Handmade from natural stone, these tiles have practical as well as aesthetic value. They are waterproof and also come with a nonslip surface that's especially good on bathroom floors and outside patios too.

Since the tile pieces are only 1 cm thick, you can apply these mosaic designs over existing tile for trimming or just

Replacing simple things like accessories and drawer/cabinet pulls will give your bathroom a whole new look. Many items are available to choose from like these with an aquatic motif. ❧

Dick Tracy Lives On
This technicolour redo looks
like it's part of the Dick
Tracy movie set, but it's
actually just a newly
decorated 1950s vintage
bathroom. The masculine
feeling suits
the man of the house just
perfectly.
Rendering by Sheryl Perry

do the shower floor[1]. First, check to see if the old tile is strongly attached by tapping around and listening for hollow sounds. Wash off the old tile with an acid to remove oil and sticky stuff. Then knock some random holes so the mosaics can bond with the old tile. Affix the new designs with a latex cement.

Q. How can I turn a boring bathroom into something interesting?

A. When you're stuck with a lack-lustre bathroom and can't stretch the budget to include a renovation, the answer is: use your imagination. This is one room you can redecorate for practically nothing. One of the most smashing make-overs I've seen was done by my friend with the cowboy bedroom, Diane Moore whom you met in *Chapter 5*. Once again, Diane turned run-of-the-mill into one-of-a-kind without professional help or any major changes.

She shifted antiques from other rooms to transform a standard apartment bathroom into a haven full of marvellous surprises. She and hubby Paul are avid collectors who made some strong statements with antiques that oozed 19th century charm — an old scale weighed out ostrich eggs and pine cones under the sink, a brass-banded rice barrel held a bird house; children's building blocks spelled out the family's names. A handsome marble-topped wash stand also provided extra storage space. Diane's sentimental fondness for hearts was incorporated on the wall hanging, guest towels and quilted pillow. A throw rug was the only new purchase.

In one tiny corner she added a lovely old chair with a soft pillow, a kerosine lamp that eliminated the need for an electrical outlet, a spot of greenery, hot coffee in bone china, and a stack of magazines — all the ingredients one needed for comfort in the cosy reading area that Diane created.

You can get the same sort of feeling with reproductions and odds and ends you gather up from other rooms in your house. The idea is to pick a theme and carry it out.

Q. Our bathroom is terribly old-fashioned but still in good condition. The colours are all wrong, and we can't afford to change anything. I'm about to give up on it.

A. Your situation is not hopeless. Stencil the wall tiles, place scented candles all around, hang pictures or framed posters, dress up corners and window sills with greenery and artificial flowers, and fill baskets with a variety of towels and magazines. You will be amazed at the results.

I hope these real-life experiences that follow will give you some ideas. Very few purchases were necessary so expenses were practically nil.

My motto is "if you can't hide it, flaunt it". When I was faced with the problems of doing up the 1950s vintage bathrooms of our colonial bungalow in Singapore, that's exactly what I did — flaunt those awful colours that I couldn't do anything about. I had to work with what was there, so I stepped back in time to the 50s and thought of ways I could make the most out of what I had.

The first bathroom I tackled was that of my husband, and it was a perfect horror! (***See rendering on page 151.***) Four different colours were used in the fixtures and tiling. The first time I looked at it, I thought, "This looks like a comic book." Immediately, my imagination jumped to Dick Tracy. So that's the theme I used.

---

1. Many building restrictions will not allow you to add anything on top of old tiles because of the increased weight. If this is the case, you must rip out existing tiles first.

S.PERRY '97

Decadent Luxury
In this bathroom a luxurious mood was created, which is described as "totally decadent". The towels and rug pick up the background colours. Old lace, silk, crystal, and scented candles add to the elegant feeling of this bathroom designed for soaking up the good life at no extra cost. Rendering by Sheryl Perry

Flaunting Retro
An antique haniwa horse,
a coordinated mixture
of rolled and stacked
towels, and plants lend
interest to out-of-the-way
spots. The colour scheme
is neatly pulled together
in the amusing
Japanese wood-block
print over the commode.
Rendering by
Sheryl Perry

Fortunately, my husband has a keen sense of humour and loved the look. He enjoyed the macho Dick Tracy and sexy Madonna images. I made a shower curtain out of some bed sheets I found in a Dick Tracy pattern and hung a clear plastic liner behind it, framed a pillow case to hang on the wall, and coordinated the towels and rugs to carry out the comic-book colours.

While patterned bed sheets-cum-shower curtains may not be available in your chosen theme, you can imitate the idea with colourful fabrics, towels and rugs. Frame a poster in lieu of a pillow case. For the final touch, add some interesting accessories.

In my bathroom (*rendering on page 153*), I created a completely different mood, which I like to call decadent luxury. The fixtures were a rosy-pink colour, the wall tiles were a matching pink, trimmed with a grey tile border, and the tiling around the tub was black — a very popular 50s colour scheme. I decided to go all the way with it.

The towels I bought picked up the pink and grey background colours and the rug was pink. At the very tall window, my husband rigged up a thin bamboo pole suspended on invisible fishing wire, and I flopped (from back to front) an old lace tablecloth over it with about a 38 cms (15 ins.) overhang to create a valance. I accessorised with artificial greenery, pink silk roses in a crystal vase, and a scented candle in a crystal candle holder. All of my favourite toiletries were placed on a shiny, white-metal tray within easy reach. The elegant feeling of that bathroom was perfect for relaxing and soaking up the good life.

The downstairs bathroom (*rendering opposite*), which also served as the guest bath, was an odd colour combination. The fixtures were medium blue; the tiles around the tub and the wall tiles were salmon; and the floor was grey tile with salmon accents. Although that sounds fairly depressing, the room turned out great in the end.

Again, I didn't try to camouflage anything except the ugly commode connections that were hidden behind an artificial

Personal and Private
Decked out in Battenberg lace and dried flowers tied up with ribbons and bows, Melinda Alexander's bathroom is her private sanctuary. The glass blocks built into an exterior wall provide plenty of natural light. Photo by Peter Mealin

plant. To give the strong-coloured wall tiles some interest, I stencilled on variegated blue morning glories with trailing green ivy. The towels were a random collection of coordinating colours; the rug and toilet seat cover were in the dominating salmon colour to match the tiles.

Finally, I added gobs of greenery in every nook and cranny, baskets for magazines and towels, and terracotta and brass accessories for texture and dimension.

Q. We need a curtain on the bathroom window for privacy, but it's always a damp and wrinkled mess. What can I do?

A. If you don't have an exhaust fan, you should install one to pull the moisture out of the bathroom. Rather than cutting a hole in the wall, I suggest fitting an exhaust fan into the window. Then cover the whole thing with a colour-coordinated, vinyl mini blind that will take the moisture. Tilt the slats for privacy when the fan is in use and, when it isn't, close the mini blinds and the fan will disappear. The blinds will stand up to frequent gentle washings with soap and water.

If you already have an exhaust fan in the wall and want something really different in the way of a window treatment, think about using glass blocks like those in the **photo on page 155.** The glass blocks are so thick that they completely distort the view inside for total privacy, which suits my friend Melinda Alexander, whom you met in previous chapters. She uses her bathroom as a personal get-away-from-it-all place where she relaxes after a hectic day at the office. She left the blocks uncovered to take full advantage of all the available light. Louvered glass slats at the top of the window that let in fresh air are neatly covered with a short curtain, which matches the one over the tub.

Q. Is it appropriate to hang pictures in the bathroom? If so,

what kind?

A. Of course you can hang whatever you want to. There are some practical guidelines though. For example, unless your bathroom is completely dry and never used for baths or showers, don't hang expensive art — it's too easily damaged by moisture. Frame inexpensive prints or posters that can be replaced if they become mildewy. A collage of amusing photographs is quite fun also. Some people like to hang nudes in the bathroom. I think that's a bit obvious, but personal preference rules on this subject.

Q. I can't stand the colour of the wall tiles. Can they be painted?

A. Yes, even glossy ceramic tiles can be painted with an oil-base or epoxy paint. The big question is how long will it last? And much depends on how well the tile walls are prepared before painting and whether or not it's a wet or dry bathroom. If it's an Asian-style bathroom with floor to ceiling wall tiles and an open shower, forget it. Anything you put on these tiles will eventually peel because of wetness.

On the other hand, if you have a tub and no shower or it's a dry bathroom with only a commode and a sink, you can try painting the tiles. You will have to be very careful when washing the floor and avoid getting the painted tiles wet. Also don't plan to wipe off the walls very often because even plain water will lift the paint sooner or later. Keep in mind that this is a temporary solution to give you time to save your money to eventually replace the tiling you don't like.

Refer to the yellow pages of the telephone book for paint companies that provide this service and check with several of them. Ask for customers' recommendations.

Q. Our little boy dropped his metal truck in the bathtub and chipped the enamel. Can it be repaired or do we have to buy a new one?

A. Depending on the amount of damage, a tub can usually be re-enamelled. For really good results, application should be done by a professional.

Q. Our bathroom floor is caked with scum and mould, and the grouting between the tiles is slimy. So ugly and dangerous too. How can I get rid of the mess or is it a hopeless situation?

A. Everyone will be happy to know there is a DIY way to solve this common problem. A bleaching powder for bathrooms and kitchens is available at any general store. Mix this powder with water until it is the consistency of

Wear all the necessary gear to protect yourself against harsh chemicals and use a long-handled brush.

paste. Before you go any further, test a small corner of the tile flooring for colour fastness. Be aware that bleaching powder may take the colour out of your tiles. Apply the mixture to the floor and leave it overnight. Be sure to wear rubber gloves to protect your hands from the bleaching power — it's strong stuff that can burn your skin.

The next day, scrub the floor ever so hard with a stiff brush. Use the kind with a long handle so you won't have to be down in the mess on your hands and knees. Check the most damaged area for cleanliness. If it isn't clean yet, leave the mixture on longer. Very bad situations may have to soak for two or three days. When you're satisfied, wash off mixture thoroughly with soap and water, then rinse well with plain water.

You may need to replace the grouting. If so, avoid using white grouting material that doesn't stay white very long. Better to match or contrast the grouting with the tile. If the tiling is white, go for an off-white, beige or grey grouting.

Q. Can I use something other than a plastic curtain on my shower stall? It gets all mildewy.

A. Any kind of plasticised, water-repellent fabric is going to collect mildew the same as an all-plastic shower curtain. The only waterproof alternative I can think of is to install a glass or plexiglass shower door, which is fine for a shower stall.

However, if a new shower door isn't what you have in mind, try washing your shower curtain. There is a way to clean the mildew off so it will look new again. Fill an automatic washing machine with water to the maximum level. Add regular detergent and a mild bleach. The amount of bleach depends upon the size of the tub — small takes about $\frac{1}{4}$ cup, medium to large about $\frac{1}{2}$ cup. It's best to start with a small amount for the first try. Then, put the plastic shower curtain in the machine and wash on the delicate or slow cycle. Be sure to test a

You can cover up a multitude of sins, including unsightly holes, with stencilled or hand-painted designs. ❧

small area for colour fastness first.

When washing by hand, follow the same procedure to this point. Let the shower curtain soak in the water to kill the mildew and mould. Wipe clean with a cloth. Hang it dripping wet in the sun to dry.

Let the machine go through the rinse cycle and remove the shower curtain before the final spin so it won't tear or wrinkle. Hang it in the sun to dry.

Q. I changed the colour scheme in the bathroom, and now the old toilet seat doesn't go. I can't find a new one that's the right colour and size. Any ideas?

A. Simply spray paint the old seat any colour you want. Use an acrylic epoxy paint in either a hi-gloss or matte finish.

Remove the seat from the toilet, then follow the directions on the paint can. Spray the first coat lightly to provide a good base for the second coat. Be sure to cover the edges. Try it — it really works.

Q. The towel racks in the bathroom were beyond salvaging, so I removed them and put the towels in baskets. I am pleased with the effect, but the holes in the tile walls are unattractive. How can I cover them up?

A. Funny you should ask this question — I was looking for a solution to the same problem in one of my old bathrooms when I saw an ad for some stencils that gave me an idea. First, I filled the holes with tile/wall cement. It has to dry thoroughly and usually more needs to be added because the compound shrinks. Then I let the creative juices flow, arranging the stencils over the holes and in a random fashion over other tiles as well. I choose a design with large flowers and leafy vines that were easy to trail over awkwardly placed holes. Even though I am not an artist and had never in my life held a paint brush, this project was fun and the results were gratifying. Try it. If at first you do not succeed, lift off the paint with a razor blade and try again.

Tip: When you can't find a stencil to your liking, you can easily make your own. First, trace a favourite design (from a magazine or whatever) onto transparent paper. Then transfer the design to a heavier paper. Cut out the design with a single-edged razor blade. If you are artistic, you can draw your own design directly onto stiff paper. ❧

Q. *I'm worried that our elderly mom will slip in the tub. Those anti-slip stick-ons aren't permanent and make a mess when they come off.*

A. There is better stuff available now. You can skid-proof slippery bathroom surfaces and also add some interest with cutouts in the shapes of fish and sea shells. Some newer stick-ons are backed with tiny suction cups so that you can move them around as needed. Good idea for little ones, too, that like to play around in the tub.

Q. *Water is running down the bathroom wall from the ceiling. We're sure it's from our neighbour's leaky tub, but he says, "No." How can we settle the argument?*

A. Use some friendly persuasion and offer to help get to the bottom of things. Once you've talked your way into his bathroom, remove the square tile cover on the opening that's close by the pipes. Stick your head in to check for traces of water around the pipes.

Then have him hold a torch all around the bathtub and the tiles. If there are any holes or cracks in the grouting or tiling, you'll see light shining through.

Q. *The chrome soapdishes and taps on the bathroom sink and shower are green and corroded. I've tried everything to clean them but nothing works. Must I replace them?*

A. You can try a couple of things before you buy new everything. Scrub all the chrome with very fine steel wool and powdered cleanser or soap-filled, steel-wool pads for cleaning pots and pans if you can find them. It takes a lot of elbow grease, but this may work if you scrub long and hard enough. I've done this myself with amazing results — 30-year-old taps looked shiny and new, for a while anyway.

There's a good possibility that they will turn green again because so much of the chrome is worn away. In that case, you can have them re-chromed. Look in the yellow pages of the telephone book for plumbing shops who provide this service. Be sure to get estimates from several because prices may vary.

Q. *The loo is located next to our lounge, and I hate bathroom noises. Is a silent-flushing toilet the answer?*

A. The once-popular symphonic (silent-flushing) toilet is down the drain because of plumbing problems. It has two traps, and if the second trap becomes obstructed, it can't be cleared. So the entire toilet has to be replaced. A better idea is a silent-filling toilet, which is easily accomplished by purchasing a special valve from an upscale bathroom-supply shop.

Q. *The powder room of our rented flat is a perfect horror. Any ideas for some quick cosmetic fixes that don't cost much?*

A. Create diversions to take the eye off the uglies like awful tile and fixtures. Put up shelving over the toilet and in corners to hold stacked towels, unusual baskets, artificial flower arrangements, interesting collections, and even framed photographs — funny photos are best because they are the most interesting.

Spring for a knock-out framed or Venetian mirror over the sink. If the budget can't stand the strain, border a plain mirror with a stencilled-on design. Go for soft lighting and lots of candles to hide glaring flaws. Fill up an attractive soap dish with colourful, decorative guest soap.

Throw a handsome rug on the floor and place a tall ceramic or terracotta water jug in the corner. Wood carvings can go on the floor next to the toilet to help hide plumbing pipes.

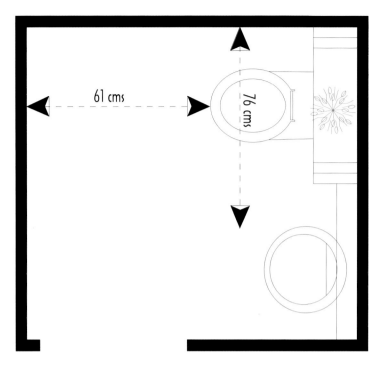

With a little effort and lots of imagination, Veena Mazumdar turned this small 1.2 x 1.2 metre (4 ft. x 4 ft.) storage closet into a lovely powder room. ❧

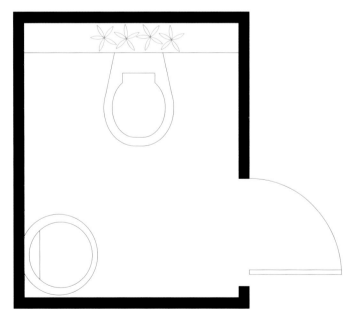

Mirrored walls visually double the size of the minuscule 0.9 x 1.2 metre (3 ft. x 4 ft.) loo in Anita Gopalakrishna's home. ❧

Pretty up the window with painted plantation shutters or bright, coordinated curtains. If the room is windowless, create the illusion of one out of a painted window-sized wood frame over a believable scene — a square or vertical poster will work. Or hang a painted Rajasthani-style window for a special effect.

Try out different ideas and move things around until it feels right.

Q. How can I turn a tacky half-bath (sink and toilet only) into a nice powder room for guests? A previous tenant already ripped off the tiles so the walls are a mess.

A. Cover up old sins quickly and cheaply by sponge painting the walls. Actually, this two- or three-toned technique works best on rough walls, and the feeling is so rustic that an amateur can handle the job. Mistakes don't matter.

Accessorise with colour everywhere — in pictures, baskets and bright towels so people won't notice structural boo-boos that aren't easy to fix. And since it's a dry bathroom, you can even put down a sisal or coir rug to cover up an ugly floor or just for fun.

If you have to replace the toilet and sink, choose a simple design in white because it's always stylish and goes with any colour combination.

Q. We have a tiny storage room under the stairs that we'd like to turn into a powder room for guests. How much space is needed?

A. You can turn the tiniest cubbyhole into a loo by using a wall-hung commode and a small-sized or corner sink. If you have as little as 1 to 1.5 square metres (12 to 16 sq. ft.) of space you can spare, you can add this important little room. You need a minimum of 76 cms (30 ins.) of unobstructed

Seashells by the Seashore
Decorated with an aquatic colour scheme in blues and white and an abundance of shells in every shape and size, Rosalie Chidwick's Indian bathroom takes on a seaside ambiance. The unused shower provides extra space for additional accessories. Photo by Rosalie Chidwick

A beautifully shaped capiz vase sits among the accessories in the unused shower. Photo by Rosalie Chidwick

More capiz-shell decorations show up in the mirror frame and the big fish over it. Photo by Rosalie Chidwick

Primitive Retreat
Yvette actually moulded the gentle curves and corners of this dressing table and seating area with her own hands. Although the shape of the white plaster built-ins has a primitive quality, the terracotta tile flooring adds a touch of warmth. Photo by the author

space around the commode and a distance of 61 cms (24 ins.) from the commode and the sink to the opposite wall. Even a space with a sloped ceiling will work when you place the commode at the low end. Trick the eye into thinking the space is bigger by hanging a big mirror or mirror a whole wall. Placing floor tiles on the diagonal seems to push the wall out.

Veena Mazumdar employed many of these ideas to add a much-needed loo to their home (***top floor plan on page 160***). She used down-sized fixtures and mounted a large mirror over the sink and display shelves over the commode. A wallpaper mural of a garden scene, giving a feeling of the outdoors, was installed on the wall opposite the door, and simply framed floral prints were hung on the wall opposite the toilet. The effect is charming.

While pocket doors are more desirable for super tiny rooms, the 1.2 metre (48 ins.) wall in Anita Gopalakrishna's loo was too short to handle one. They opted for a narrow door that opened outwards because they felt the bathroom was too cramped for the door to be hinged on the inside, which is the norm.

Anita made additional visual expansions by mirroring the wall behind the sink and also the wall behind the commode. Then she had Lucite display shelves installed above the commode that are nicely reflected in the mirrors.

Q. Our guest bathroom has an Asian-style shower in it that we never use. How can I disguise it?

A. Don't try to hide it. Decorate it like interior designer Rosalie Chidwick did. She used the shower area as an

Looking Good ▶
A previously nondescript loo and entrance space in a modern flat was transformed by Gill Hough when she combined some of her collected Asian treasures with her innate sense of what's right. Photo by Pallon Daruwala

*Uninteresting corner
before transformation.*

Sitting Pretty
*Proportion and colour are the
decorating elements that
filled up this previously naked
corner.*
Rendering by Sheryl Perry ❧

opportunity to hang additional fabric, draped to resemble a shower curtain. The more fabric you hang in a tile bathroom to muffle the sound, the better.

To accent the all-white tiles and walls, Rosalie chose various shades of blue. The previously dead-looking bathroom came alive with colour and the eye-catching shell motif. Notice how the stencilled-on shell border completes the floor-to-ceiling decor (**photos on page 161**).

Q. My husband and I are mad for good art and want it all over the house. I'd like to put something in the guest bath, but what about mildew, dampness and such?

A. Oils are definitely a no-no since they're unsealed and open to moisture. Water colours and expensive prints should be mounted on acid-free paper and sealed for protection, so if the bathroom is not actually used for bathing or showering, it's a maybe.

I just had to hang a rather pricey piece in our guest bath because it's so right for the room. I check it at least once a week for any warping or curling and look behind it for signs of dampness. In two years time, nothing has happened.

Before you try it, have your framer update the condition of the mounting[1]. Get their advice too.

Q. Our old bungalow has a very large bathroom, and we're wondering what to do with all the space. Can you help us?

A. Several things come to mind. If the bathroom is a fairly dry area, line the walls with shelving for books and knick-knacks. Add a comfortable chair and side table to make a quiet reading spot. Another idea is to use the extra space for a makeup centre like that in a restored bungalow near Mysore, owned by a fascinating woman known only as Yvette.

Q. How can I hide an ugly exhaust fan that is set into the bathroom window?

A. The simplest way is to cover it up like Gill Hough did. She had a fan just as you described in the guest loo of her flat and found it as unsightly as you do. To hide it, Gill did a super attractive window treatment with soft, flowing white crisscrossed tie-backed curtains with a *dupatta* draped over it, forming a valance.

Although the loo is tiny, she still finds room to tuck in some accessories that are both useful and decorative. For example, the elephant provides a spot to stack extra hand towels, and the small chest holds odds and ends. The total picture is most effective (**photo on page 163**).

Q. Our bathroom has one empty corner that looks "naked." I can't hang anything on the walls because they are covered with marble tiling, and I don't want to knock holes. How can I decorate this little space?

A. The **rendering opposite** shows the before-and-after look of a corner decoration that defies the allotted space. The chair is tall and very narrow so it fits snugly next to a small chest. What looks like black Italian marble trim is actually a thin film of faux-marble celluloid that is simply stuck onto the plain white marble walls. This added touch and the magenta-coloured artificial flowers in a shiny brass vase and a brass bowl of showy potpourri make a bright decoration that makes up for the lack of wall hangings.❧

---

1. Mounting: refers to the total framing treatment which includes the mat (border), glass, frame, acid-free backing, and regular backing (usually wood) — whatever is used.

CHAPTER 8

Window Treatments

INTRODUCTION

Window dressing, like the rest of home decorating, goes through phases. Over the years trends have included everything from elaborate multi-layered treatments to unadorned Venetian blinds[1]. I remember that latter phase all too well — when white, metal Venetian blinds were the rage and used throughout the house regardless of decor. No one wanted to cover them up, except in posh living and dining rooms where awful side panels or pleated draw drapes were sometimes added as an attempt at formality.

Unhappily, lots of yesterday's draw drapes are still around simply because many people don't know what else to do. Or because they think it's too difficult and costly to deal with proper window treatments, and unfortunately that used to be all too true. The big difference between yesterday and today is a more imaginative approach to window treatments that doesn't have to cost the earth. Now there's a wider variety of looks to choose from. Drapes and curtains aren't the only way to go anymore and sometimes aren't necessary at all. Simple, painted window frames, blinds of all types, stand-alone swags, and unadorned lacy sheers are among today's fashionable alternatives. Traditional multi-layered treatments are still around, sporting a new look of exciting colours, fabrics and styles.

Up-to-date window treatments will give your whole house a face-lift and take it into the future with panache! Read on for lots of ideas for tackling all kinds of window dilemmas, including hard-to-handle shapes and sizes, what to do with curtains that are past their prime, and how to get smashing new looks without spending too much.

------

1. Venetian blinds: a blind made of horizontal slats, which adjust to let in light and air. So named because they came from Italy more than 200 years ago.

Q. We're setting up our first house, and I don't know what to do with the windows. How do I know what will look good?

A. Since window treatments can make or break an entire room, you will want to give careful thought to this important part of decorating. You should not hurry through the selection process. The idea is to incorporate the window treatments with the architectural style of your home and your over-all decorating scheme.

After you take stock of what you're working with, make up a file folder of magazine pictures that catch your fancy. When you use decorating books that can't be cut up, make sketches and notes about the things you like to add to your folder.

The job of selecting the colours and fabrics for the windows is made easier by settling on upholstery fabrics first, so do up the rooms and leave the windows to last. I have been known to have bare windows for months in my own home, hanging up cast-off curtains for privacy in the bedrooms, while I shop and think about what's right. Bed sheets temporarily tacked over the top of window frames will work too.

Q. What kinds of window treatments are good here and which ones should I stay away from?

A. Generally speaking, an uncomplicated style is best for India's climate, architecture and the expansive glass windows found in many newer apartments. Any of the treatments suggested in this chapter's **Introduction** are not only good, they're terrific!

Heavy drapes, ornate valances and elaborate window treatments should be used sparingly and only in large rooms because they can overpower the decor to the detriment of small rooms, making the rooms seem even smaller. Also it's difficult and costly to maintain great expanses of draperies.

But I won't say that you should stay away from them entirely because there are some rooms that scream for over-the-top window dressings, and I personally have used them in our Bangalore home. Most drapery and curtain treatments will work anywhere when they get updated with fashionable fabrics and styling that is in keeping with the decor. It's the tired, same old thing that doesn't fly anymore.

However, don't limit yourself to just curtains and drapes. Used by themselves or as under-treatments, blinds are especially versatile for getting a huge variety of looks. From fancy Austrian blinds to functional roller blinds, there are styles and colours to fit in almost any place.

Austrian blinds are good for windows that require more dressing up (*photo opposite*). Fabric is vertically ruched (gathered) to create gentle swags when the blind is let down. When it's pulled up, the gentle swags become quite pouffy.

Balloon blinds (aka festoons) are similar to Austrian blinds except they aren't vertically ruched. The heading is either gathered or pleated using an inverted pleating method, which results in a more tailored look. The bottom of the shade poufs like a blown-up balloon as the blind is raised.

Balloon blinds work in most medium and lightweight fabrics and are especially well-suited for lace, but you won't get so much of the billowing effect with limper fabrics. They should be left unlined when done in lace to allow the light to play through the pattern. Other sheer fabrics should also be left unlined when using balloons or Austrian blinds as elegant sun shades or screens to mask a dreary view (*page 170, top*).

Over the Top ▶
A dramatic Austrian blind is just the right touch for the theatrical treatment that was designed to hold down the strong architectural features of this dining room. Done in a semi-sheer, unlined fabric, the blind works as a sun screen when it's lowered during the afternoons but doesn't completely block the pleasant garden view.
Photo by Pallon Daruwala ❧

Roman blinds (*below*) are one of the most adaptable and fashionable treatments around. They can either blend with the wall when the setting calls for it or become a striking feature in an otherwise drab room. They can stand alone for a clean, uncluttered look or work as the foundation for a multi-layered window dressing. They are good for just about any room, especially studies and boys' bedrooms for a smooth, tailored look. They work very well in small rooms because they give you the opportunity to use windows as walls for furniture placement without the messy look of mashed up drapes. They are custom made to fit any window in any colour and theme to suit you, but they get too heavy to pull up if they're much wider than 135 cms (54 ins.). Any fabric can be used except one that's too thick, like a tapestry, because it won't fold properly.

Aluminium rods are inserted for flat, even folds when the blind is raised. Choose a substantial, but not bulky, fabric that will take the stress of being pulled up and down. Flimsy material won't do because it will stretch. Protect the fabric from sun damage with a lining.

Venetian and mini blinds[1] (*opposite, top*) are great sun blocks, durable and easy to wipe clean. They are especially well suited for bathrooms where the curtains go limp and mildewy and kitchens that get grimy with grease. But they don't work on big sliding doors and aren't quite right on French doors.

Luxaflex Duette honeycomb blinds by Hunter Douglas®, manufactured now in India, are the newest way to treat all types of windows. They work with any decor from contemporary (*opposite, bottom right*) to country and are perfect for odd-shaped windows (*opposite, bottom far right*). For even more flexibility, Duette shades can be installed to work three ways — from the top-down, bottom-up, or both ways at the same time. They are amazingly easy to

Balloon blinds. Rendering by Sheryl Perry 🕭

A Roman blind fits snugly against the window frame in this cosy reading corner in Robert Mathis's flat. Photo by Pallon Daruwala 🕭

---

1. Mini blinds: made like Venetian blinds but with narrower horizontal slats.

Top: **Luxaflex mini blinds are available in wide range of colours to coordinate with any theme. Photo courtesy of Hunter Douglas® and Window Furnishing India Pvt. Ltd.**

Right: **Luxaflex Duettes by Hunter Douglas® work well in a sleek contemporary setting. Photo courtesy of Hunter Douglas® and Window Furnishing India Pvt. Ltd.**

Extreme right: **Unadorned blinds cover an arched window and the tall window below in a matched, classical style. The arched blind is non-operational. Photo courtesy of Hunter Douglas® and Window Furnishing India Pvt. Ltd.** ❧

operate and so strongly constructed that they won't sag, even with a 4.27 metre (14 ft.) expanse. They can stand alone or provide the background for a multi-layered treatment.

I've heard complaints that dirt gets trapped in the honeycombs, but surprise, surprise — most duettes are washable. **Be sure to read the instructions first or check with the dealer.**

Of course, the convenience of a product that solves all your window decorating problems does not come cheaply. Duettes are definitely a luxury item for the well-heeled and are expensive. But guaranteed to impress one and all.

Don't overlook the humble *chik*. They have caught on and are very in vogue in the West. When used in a casual setting with rattan, Rajasthani and/or colonial antique furniture, they make a fashion statement. Spray-paint *chiks* and line them with cheap matching cotton. Or use them *au naturel*, lined with unbleached muslin. Trim the edges with wide decorative ribbon to tie in with your colour scheme.

For a very original treatment, you can go with asymmetric curtains, tie backs, drapes, uneven swags (***illustration No. 5, page 184***), or fish tails (***illustration No. 4, page 184***). For drama, try swagging a beautiful *dupatta*[1], or a cotton or silk sari over a decorative pole. These looks are becoming very popular and people take to them once they know about them.

Q. How do I know how much fabric to buy?

A. The first step is deciding whether you're going to use plain rods, traverse rods[2] or poles to hold up the curtains or

drapes. Ideally, the hardware should be in place before you measure for length. The heights of the rods and poles will vary according to preference, styling, and need — for example, when you need to make a window look longer, the hardware must be raised higher than normal. If you're using wall-to-wall carpeting or room-sized rugs, they also should be in place to measure for full-length treatments. In other

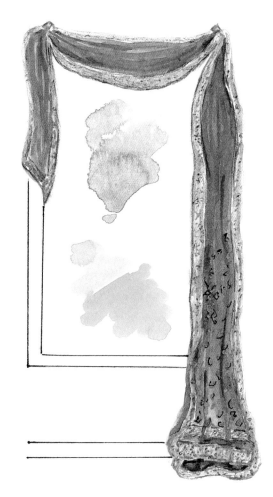

A gorgeous silk sari hung asymmetrically is an easy elegant treatment. Rendering by Sheryl Perry ❧

---

1. *Dupatta:* a long rectangular shawl.
2. Traverse rods: type of rod used for draw drapes. Available for two-panel centre pull and one-panel left or right pull.

words, you must know what you're working towards and the look you want to achieve before accurate measurements can be taken by you or a drapery person. There's much more to it than simply measuring the height and width of the window.

The finished length includes the overlap for the heading and a nice, deep hem of 10 to 15 cms (4 to 6 ins.) which you must insist on. (I find that many drapery people try to skimp on hems.) Allow at least 5 cms (2 ins.) for side seams. Another point you must insist on is that 12 mm ($\frac{1}{2}$ in.) of fabric is turned under the heading, bottom and side hems to hide the selvages and unfinished edges. If you're having sheers or unlined curtains and drapes made, the panel seams must also be turned under and finished neatly.

Pleated and gathered styles must be generously full — usually two to three times the length of the rod. Formal effects like box and cartridge pleats take more. Too little fabric looks flat and meagre. If your budget doesn't stretch far enough to do up curtains and drapes in the right way, it's better to go without them and opt for less expensive alternatives.

> *Tip: Drapery makers frequently try to save time and labour by cutting corners and slapping things together, and that just won't do. Don't let them get away with saying, "That's the way it's done." Remember: you're a paying customer, and you have the right to demand the best workmanship.*❧

Q. I don't want to make mistakes by choosing curtain fabrics and colours that will quickly go out of style. What's popular now, and what can we expect in the near future?

A. The trend is going away from dominating colours and moving towards more muted shades in the same tones. Lots of strong yellows are popping up somewhere in patterned fabrics. Earth tones are on the scene again, thanks to the ecology movement, but there's new dimension to the colours. Softer jewel tones are big. These are the *in* colours now that will get stronger as we look to the future. Blues aren't a good choice, not from lack of popularity but because they fade faster in strong sunlight than any other colour. Greens are next, then reds. Down and out of favour are very pale pastels and nondescript beiges.

Patterns are also inspired by nature; florals are garden and botanical prints. Animal prints are very much in fashion. While I don't suggest them for expansive window treatments, they're great on fabric-covered roller blinds or Roman blinds in kids' rooms and studies. Geometrics are in plaids, stripes, tribal designs, and Indian-inspired colours and patterns.

Q. Is it better to use natural fabrics or are synthetic materials okay too?

A. Fabrics in natural fibres like cotton and linen last longer than synthetics when well cared for. They should be dry-cleaned periodically and vacuum dusted every week or two so dust doesn't get a chance to settle into the fibres. Natural fabrics are revived after cleaning and have a fresh, almost new look. Dye permeates the threads of natural fibres, and once the dust is removed, the colour returns. Don't vacuum fragile fibres like silk, delicate lace and sheers because the sucking action breaks down the fibres. Ask your decorator for cleaning recommendations. If vacuumed regularly, once a year professional cleaning should be enough.

Synthetic and polyester fabrics are damaged by the sun and fade because the threads only take colour on the surface. Dust corrodes and destroys the fibres too. Not a good choice for India's weather.

Tip: Windows in bungalows should be treated differently from those in high-rise apartment buildings because the lighting is not the same. There's more outside greenery visible from bungalows, so you might choose stronger colours and patterns. Blend window treatments with the natural view for the best effect. Use softer colours and patterns for high-rises, keeping the look lighter and brighter. Think of window dressings as picture frames for pleasant views. When the view is not worth looking at, blur the picture with a screening effect that doesn't cut out all the light.

Q. What are blackout linings and do I need them?

A. Blackout linings are made of a special synthetic material that blocks light. If you are a light sleeper and wake up at the crack of dawn, or your kids do, you need them in your bedrooms. But don't use them in the living room where normal linings are usually enough. They are available in different colours, and although black and silver probably keep out the biggest amount of light, they are heavy and stiff and don't draw nicely. White is the softest and easiest to work with. Blackouts cost two to three times more than regular linings, and there are other less expensive ways to block light.

When your colour scheme allows for darker colours at the windows, you can opt for black, dark brown or burgundy coloured mini blinds or simple roller blinds. Combined with over-drapes, these options are quite effective and blackout linings aren't necessary. Or if you have a gutsy approach to decorating, you can use my idea (*right*) that worked to darken our movie room, even in broad daylight. Mounted on a fixed rod, the black silk under-panels are lined with regular, black lining fabric and held back from the centre with cording. For daytime movie viewing, I simply release the cords and the under-curtain drops closed. One can, of course, release the lined, silk over-drapes (also mounted on a fixed rod), but this usually is not necessary.

Lights Out
Black under-curtains, lined with black fabric shut out daylight in this movie room. Dark-coloured drapes lined with black fabric work too. **Photos by Pallon Daruwala**

Q. How can I keep the sun from ruining our furniture and still be able to see out?

A. Sheers are good sun screens. They filter light without completely blocking the view. And they make for a versatile treatment whether you choose a simple stand-alone window dressing or get a fancy layered treatment like this

Fancy layered sheers.
Rendering by Sheryl Perry

illustration (*left*). The under-curtain is a single, weighted[1] panel, which can be gathered onto a fixed rod because you won't be opening the curtain to over-expose your furniture. To get the right effect for the draped and swagged valance, use two different colours of sheer fabric — one to match the panel and another for accent. The pair are held at the top by brackets, and the sides are knotted together about $\frac{1}{3}$ the way from the bottom.

Q. How much should I budget for window treatments?

A. You will need about 10% to 20% of your decorating budget. If you're starting with a new or newly renovated home, figure 10% to 20% of the total cost of the interior design, which includes everything you add to the interior like kitchen cabinets, appliances, wardrobes, flooring, rugs and carpets, furniture, lighting and bathroom fixings. For example, Rs 20,000 to Rs 40,000 is the right proportion for a two-lakh interior. When you're just redoing window treatments, it depends on how much you can afford, doesn't it? Plan to spend the most on the public rooms, the living room and dining room, and pamper yourself in the main bedroom. Cut corners in the kitchen and bathroom. If you must, economise in the children's bedrooms with less expensive treatments.

Of course, you can spend less and still get great, put-together looks. Go for swags, tails and asymmetric styles that call for less fabric, and tie-back curtains over roller blinds rather than multiple layers of drapes. Use a neighbourhood shop for simple curtains, and use a professional only for unique treatments.

---

1. Weights: either small triangular-shaped metal pieces tucked into the corner of a curtain hem or a string of tiny metal beading, place inside the hem that runs the length of the curtain panel.

Q. What is a curtain specialist?

A. While most fabric shops can sew up curtains, it takes a curtain specialist to advise suitable treatments that work best with your interior. They know the latest trends, colours and styles. Naturally, these specialists are found in decorator shops that aren't among the cheapest in town. Their treatments can be time consuming to make so the labour charges are higher. You're also paying for their expertise, designer fabrics, the latest fashions, and custom hardware. On the other hand, if you're stuck in the multi-layered mode, a specialist can save you money by introducing new, less complicated ideas.

Q. I want to give my old draw drapes a new look. What can I do that won't cost a lot of money?

A. Add a valance that is softly shaped and draped on a decorator pole. Use a fabric that coordinates with your existing drapes. For example, if your drapes are a solid colour, use a patterned fabric or a striped, checked or plaid fabric for the valance. If your drapes are in a figured fabric, use a solid colour for the valance. Select a type of fabric for the valance that is compatible with the drapes, cotton with cotton, silk or brocade with silk, and so forth. Take a drapery panel with you when you shop for the new fabric.

Tie the old drapery panels back with tasselled cording. Use braided cords and tassels in co-ordinating colours. Tie backs should be done up one-third of the way from bottom of the curtain — never half-way.

Tip: Lined curtains and drapes always hang better than unlined. Valances and panels need linings for additional body and to protect against sun damage. Attach a light-weight lining to the heading and side seams of the drapes, leaving the bottom hem loose to allow some manoeuvring space in case either of the fabrics shrink when dry-cleaned or washed.

Q. What kind of style is good for a cosy look that's not too homey?

A. Go for a simple casual style that gives a friendly feeling (***below***). It works well with wrought-iron or rattan furniture and antique accent pieces. This treatment depends upon a free and easy fabric, like cotton or voile, and an artistically designed pole for successful definition. Fabric loops are fed onto the wrought-iron pole for manual opening and closing. If privacy is a factor or you're covering east or west windows that get direct sunlight, use a roller blind underneath. The fabric loops will be damaged eventually if you have to close the curtains too often.

Tip: When using a patterned fabric for simple curtains, add a plain border to form a background and give dimension to the curtain panels.

Casual styling. Rendering by Sheryl Perry

Q. *I want formal-looking curtains for our hall but can't think of anything different from the usual drapes and sheers. Can you suggest something?*

A. A lot depends on the room and the type of window. A truly formal treatment makes a strong statement and needs space to carry it off. Higher-than-normal ceilings and big, tall windows take to this treatment. Having said all that, I'll immediately qualify it by saying that there are ways you can get the look by modifying it. For example, the ***photo below*** shows a formal style that's adaptable to most settings.

The semi-sheer panels are pleated for nice deep folds and can be hung on a draw rod if you need to open them for light or air. The swagged, silk valance fashioned with fish tails is on a fixed rod. This flexible treatment works on both small and large windows and can go either short (just below the window sill) or long (to the floor).

The second adaptation is one that I designed for my husband's study in our Bangalore home and broke all the rules in doing so (***below***). The room is relatively small, 4.25 x 3.35 metres (13.8 x 10.9 ft.), with a 3-metre (9.8 ft.) ceiling, and a wide arched window that looked rather squatty.

First, I raised the brass decorator pole to just below the crown moulding to add height to the window. Then I

A formal look can work in a small room when it doesn't compete with a lot of accessories.
Photo by Pallon Daruwala

This adaptable formal look works for both sill-length and full-length treatments. Photo by Pallon Daruwala

decided on a heavy brocade fabric for the valance that was done in box pleats and hung on brass rings. The valance is extra deep and proportioned correctly so nobody knows its actually hiding the wall above the window. To mimic the arch I covered up, the bottom of the valance is curved. In fact, you can use this technique to get an arched effect on regular windows.

Because light is an important factor in a study, I chose a net-like fabric for the panels and bordered them with the brocade to match the valance for a truly smashing look. However, I must admit that the border wasn't in the original plan. I only came up with it as a solution to a problem — the sewers had cut the panels too short! (I don't know who said, "Necessity is the mother of invention," but it's so true.)

For a really formal effect, I put a long flowing fringe on the valance and added cording and tassels to break up the long expanse of the too-wide window. A traverse rod wasn't called for because cording ties back the panels from the centre.

The best thing about this design is its versatility. For example, you may want to use an elegant silk or brocade fabric for the whole treatment. If your pocketbook won't handle quite that much elegance, you can get the same feeling with a dressy, patterned chintz or a swishy-looking, heavy cotton fabric. In any case, when you use the same fabric for both the valance and panels, you must add a significant border or a serious fringe to the valance to define its shape and set it apart from the panels. And no skimping on fabric is allowed because the drapes must be full and floor length to handle such a dramatic valance. You can also add plain under-sheers to hide ugly window frames and not-so-nice views.

Tip: Don't mix formal window treatments with casual or modern furniture or contemporary themes.

Q. I need an unfussy idea for a simply furnished room.

A. Fabric covered roller blinds are a flat, minimal look that works well on regular to small windows and in rooms where you can't give up the space for a fuller treatment. They are the practical, economical approach to window covering where privacy and protection from the sun is needed. They can stand alone for a no fuss look or can be dressed up with over-curtains — but stay simple to keep the relaxed mood that's compatible with roller blinds.

Striped fabrics work especially well and scallops, deep points and triangles are interesting shapes for the bottom line. Go big and bold rather than small and insignificant if you decide to use a contoured edge.

Q. What are neo-classic window treatments? I've seen the term in decorating magazines but can't imagine what it looks like.

A. The neo-classic trend in home decorating was the rage all through the 90s and is still a popular way to do up windows. Favourite patterns are mostly Roman anything, including urns, jugs, columns, and lots of heads. They are bold and need space to show off, but the look has versatility. It's perfect for traditional and post-modern settings. You can go with the full drapery treatment, but that's rather pricey because the fabric is expensive and usually has a big pattern repeat. You may want to evoke the feeling with less complicated treatments like Roman blinds with deep swags and tails, or simple no-pull panels over the blinds.

Black and white is the favourite colour combination, but burgundy and cream, and softer hues are good options. The pattern design is the important factor in setting the classic mood (*rendering opposite*).

If mod is your goal, you need drama colour combos like red and black or maroon and grey for a softer look. Solids are best, but masculine-looking stripes with a solid lining will also work. The mini blinds should match the colour of the lining to avoid confusion. When necessary, you can visually widen regular-sized windows by extending the decorator pole over the wall space on both sides.

To get the asymmetric effect, the pinned-back drapery panel is twice the width of the other panel. Shallow pleats all across the top allows the fabric to fall gracefully from curtain rings and are better for this look than conventional pleating techniques.

Make the job of doing up your windows easy by adapting the same style in your bedroom, using a different colour combination.

Neo-classic styling. Rendering by Sheryl Perry

Q. I'm a single guy whose job has got me transferred away from home. What kind of drama thing can I do in my new bachelor pad?

A. Go for a knock-their-socks-off window treatment in your living room with this new twist to the layered look (**right**). Here's how: flip back a coordinated lining to show off the other side of a drapery panel. Use mini blinds to back up this dramatic treatment that works for wide windows in contemporary to traditional settings, depending on your choice of fabrics and colours.

Modern and contemporary settings can carry dramatic window treatments when the styling is faithful to the mood. Rendering by Sheryl Perry

Tip: Knee-highs don't work. Full-length drapes and curtains must at least "kiss" the floor, and shorties[1] must hang well below the window sill to look good. Those that stop short look skimpy.❧

Q. I love the café curtains in our kitchen and would like to use them in the baby's room. Is this okay or are they meant for the kitchen only?

A. When café curtains first made their way into homes during the 1950s and 60s, they were found most often in kitchens and informal eating areas because the idea originated in cafés where they were hung on the bottom half of the window to protect seated patrons from prying eyes — hence the name. However, those days are long gone, and now this versatile style is being used all over the house.

Café curtains will go in your baby's room very success-fully to fit in with any theme, depending on the shape of the valance and the type of fabric. One time I adapted the style to work in with a circus theme for our little girl's room. I used a wide pink and white striped cotton fabric and shaped the valance to resemble a circus tent. If your baby is a boy, you can use the same idea with stronger-coloured fabric. The top of the valance was gathered onto a flat rod, and about 15.24 to 20.32 cms (6 to 8 ins.) from the bottom another pocket was stitched so it could be gathered onto a curved rod for effect. If a custom-made rod isn't in the budget, a standard rod will do. But it should have at least a 10 cms (4 ins.) elbow to hold the valance away from the window frame. I scalloped the bottom of the valance. The café panels were nearly flat, about 1.5 times the width of the window. Brass rings were sewn on so the panel could slide open and shut easily. To block the light, I added a black-out

Café curtains with a circus theme are perfect for young children's bedrooms. Rendering by Sheryl Perry ❧

Café au Lait ▶
Café curtains go formal when done in silk with draped over-panels. Photo by Pallon Daruwala ❧

---

1. Shorties: window-sill length curtains and drapes.

roller blind behind the curtains.

Here you see it done in one of my bedrooms as a full window treatment for arched windows (**photo on page 181**). The silk over-drapes are gathered onto a fixed rod and pulled back from the centre with cording and tassels. The cafés themselves are also in silk with pleated headings hung from brass rings. For effect and to balance the weight of the heavy over-drapes, I chose a big fat brass decorator pole.

> *Tip: Cotton and silk voile are great fabric alternatives to boring nylon sheers. Voile is thin and diaphanous and so light that it seems to float. A semi-transparent fabric, it just barely veils the view when used as a window covering and softens an opulent drapery treatment when it goes underneath in a multi-layered look. You can also use yards and yards of voile to swathe a curtain pole and let the ends drip down the sides of the window into puddles. Use your imagination to create a dreamy look with this easy to work with fabric.*

Q. Are lace curtains too old-fashioned-looking to use these days?

A. The cool and breezy look of lace curtain panels continues to be a perennial favourite, especially in warm-weather climates. The lace filters light without blocking the air flow. This treatment is best on windows that don't get direct sunlight and where privacy isn't a factor.

Outside light is important to get the full benefit of lace. The delicate patterns appear to be suspended in space when lit from behind. But light also outlines the shape of the window, so good frames are a must.

Lace comes in a variety of patterns, everything from traditional florals to modern geometrics, so it's easy to select something suitable for any theme or style. Although some laces are very pricey, you can capture the same feeling with much less expensive fabric if you are careful to allow for

shrinkage. Hand wash the fabric before having curtains made up.

Q. My curtains are so uninteresting and need up-dating, but I can't afford to throw them away. Do you have any ideas for refurbishing the old ones?

A. It isn't necessary to throw out the old curtains and start over. Thanks to today's styling, there are countless ways to recycle your original investment when you get bored with what you have. These new looks also work well if you're moving house and are stuck with curtains that don't fit — and it seems like they never do. Refer to the following descriptions and illustrations for lots of helpful ideas.

1. Two for One: use an old multi-layered treatment from one window to cover two new windows. If the panels are already pleated, hang them from rings. If they are flat, gather them onto an ordinary double rod. Put one drapery panel on the outside all the way across the window and tie it back. The old sheer goes underneath, hung the same way and tied back on the other side of the window. *Voilà!* You have the other half of the old treatment to do up another window.

2. A Smoothy: a single curtain, fixed flat across the top of the window and drawn to one side with a diagonal drawstring turns old linen, heavy cotton or canvas material into a fresh modern style. Bold patterns work better than stripes, but stay casual. Hang from a decorator rod to add interest to this super easy treatment.

3. Sheer Delight: copy this look by using two different patterns of full sheers or cotton voile in the same colour. A single long panel is tied back with a cord. Overhanging this, another panel forms a delicate swag for the valance before falling in a straight line to the floor. Dainty ball fringe unites the mismatched panels and adds form but not weight.

A variation on this theme allows for panels in different colours. For example, combining white and ecru or pastels and cream lets you use up odds and ends. Use the darker colour for the pelmets.

4. Swags and Fishtails: old drapes can be re-tailored for a more modern approach to traditional looks. Fishtails and swag are bordered and hung from a decorator rod. The look is formal, but it's a dressed-down version that fits in with today's styling.

A drape, swag and fishtails were fashioned from old curtain panels to get this treatment which is especially suited for long windows and French doors that open out. Extend the decorator pole over the wall on one side to accommodate the drape. Tie it back with a braided cord to keep it out of the way.

5. Asymmetric Shorty: brass rings and heavy cord trimming add eye-catching appeal to this brief little ditty that works for windows of all sizes. Use a substantial fabric to counterbalance the weight of the brass curtain rings and the trim. Simply mount the rings on the wall or window frame and run the fabric through them. Be sure the fabric is wide enough to allow for generous draping, but the length is up to your personal taste.

6. Ribbons and Bows: use your existing drapes just the way they are and add some bows to get this swishy new look. Tie back the panels one-fourth the distance from the top. Then blouse the mid-section and place the next set of bows one-third the distance from the bottom. The treatment also works on French doors that open outwards. Raise the curtain rod well above the door frame.

7. A Cinch: shut out the sun and get some privacy without blocking the light by cinching in sheers, voile, lace, or thin muslin at the waist. Tie up with pretty bows. Fix the curtains flush against doors and you can use this treatment with doors that open in or out. A great way to use up old under panels.

8. Modern Interpretations: formal-looking treatments don't have to go all the way to the floor these days. In this illustration, the drapes come just below the window sill. The two panels are parted in the centre and pulled back over curtain holders barely one-fourth the distance from the top for this updated classic look. The sides should be pulled straight, and the centre portion of the panels are allowed to drape which shapes the bottoms as well. It's a good way to use up old draperies that aren't long enough for floor-length window treatments. Use with or without cornice board.

9. A Frame Up: frame the top and sides of the window with cornice boards covered in old drapery fabric. You need a heavy material because it must be stretched tight. Boards can be padded with foam rubber for an upholstered look. The treatment can stand alone or it can take under sheers.

10. Something Out Of Nothing: you can use any old thing for this casual approach to formal dressing. Even an old bedspread or a long tablecloth will work. A fancy rod is nice but not absolutely necessary — an inexpensive wood pole will do just as well. If you use something plain-coloured, a little trimming or short fringe on the edges adds interest.

11. Get Looped: you can get this imaginative look with valances by threading the tops and ends of sheer panels on an ordinary rod. Cut the old sheers to the desired length, allowing plenty of fabric for finished top and bottom hems, which will be the part that the rod goes through. You have a choice of two different looks. One way is to lay the sheers

1. Two for One

2. A Smoothy

3. Sheer Delight

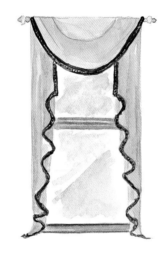

4. Swags and Fishtails

5. Asymmetric Shorty

6. Ribbons and Bows

7. A Cinch

Renderings by Sheryl Perry 🍃

8. *Modern*
   Interpretations

9. *A Frame*
   Up

10. *Something*
    out of Nothing

11. *Get Looped*

12. *Pleasantly Peasant*

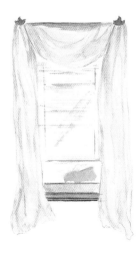

13. *Easy Does It*

14. *Clean and*
    Fresh

Renderings by Sheryl Perry

with the right side of the fabric facing you. Threading top and bottom hems onto the rod from this position, the panels form a horseshoe.

The second option is to thread the top of the sheer panel onto the rod with the right side of the fabric facing you. Then form a loop by threading the bottom hem onto the rod with the wrong side of the fabric facing you. Sheers are ideal for this because the front and back look the same.

Hang the new valance over a pair of curtains. Use a traverse rod for the under panels so you can close them for privacy. If that's not a problem, you can hang them on a regular rod and tie them back from the centre to let in light. The treatment can go either short or long and is super on big glass sliding doors and attractive casement windows.

Panels and valances don't have to be the same colour, but when you go for a colour combo, use the darker one for the valance.

12. Pleasantly Peasant: sheets or muslin are best for Eastern European peasant dressing. It works short or long on a regular to wide window. Pull the centre of the material above the window and twist it into a knot. Pin the sides back up high, leaving the top corners of the window exposed or not — depending on your personal preference. The look goes Middle Eastern with sheets in appropriate patterns or striped canvas.

13. Easy Does It: a long single piece of flat fabric is all you need for an elegant, but so simple, curtain. The swag is held up on both sides of the window by curtain holders and the sides are allowed to fall freely to the floor for the full treatment. But the look works as a shorty, too. If your leftover fabric isn't long enough, you can piece it together at the top corners. The curtains can stand alone or you can use Duettes, roller shades or mini blinds underneath.

14. Clean and Fresh: all-cotton terry cloth towels make great, easy-care bathroom curtains. Pre-wash new towels to allow for shrinkage before sewing them up. The pelmet is flat and just gathered onto an ordinary double rod. Panels are hung behind the pelmet and pulled shut by hand. They should be full enough to cover the window with gentle gathers. Add lace trimming for a finished look.

Q. The windows of our flat are covered with grills which are needed for security but ugly to look at. How can I disguise them?

A. Paint the grills white and they will almost disappear during the day. If you're still not satisfied, cover the windows with a white semi-transparent or lace treatment. For the best nighttime effect go for an over-curtain, lined in white, that closes. Even from the outside, the grills will blend in with the under sheers and white curtain lining so they're hardly noticeable.

Q. Our flat is small and very ordinary. What style of curtains should I get for the living room?

A. It's best to do simple window treatments in small rooms with normal ceilings. Too fussy or elaborate will look overdone. But simple doesn't mean boring! It just means that small rooms look best when the windows aren't the main features. Instead, you should set the style with the furniture and accessories, then do up the windows to blend in. A few suggestions: Roman shades are good for an informal setting; semi-sheers with pulled back over-curtains go classic or cosy depending on the fabric; and, though I'm usually not keen on mini blinds in the living room, it's an effective look with contemporary and hi-tech decor — especially done in matt-finish silver or grey.

Q. *For the sake of privacy, my living room windows need the full treatment. Can I keep the cost down and get a designer look too?*

A. Yes, because you don't need a full layered effect that requires yards and yards of expensive fabric to protect yourself from prying eyes. Use one of the many kinds of blinds that are available to provide necessary privacy. You can make them work with any type of decor.

Roman shades take on different looks depending on the kind of fabric and trimming that's used. You can go very simple with canvas which works well in a casual tropical setting. Wide stripes go sporty. Brocades and silks are more formal. Most any fabric that folds up smoothly will do. Edges can be plain, scalloped or trimmed with fancy braids and fringe.

Venetian blinds come in widths that range from micro mini to extra wide. Colours run the gamut from glitzy metallic to subtle matt finishes, and the very latest — wooden slats preferably in extra wide that's wonderful with regional,

rustic, soft country, and English library looks.

Another treatment calls for swags or side panels topped off with a valance. Back them up with pull-down roller blinds made in a co-ordinating fabric.

Q. *Our living/dining area has a top hung and a sliding window located side-by-side on one wall. Will window-sill curtains of different lengths look awful?*

A. Well, maybe not awful but there are other solutions that will definitely look better. Even things up by making the two windows appear to be the same length (**below**). Here's how: on the wall below the top hung window, attach either a layer of fixed shutters or decorative wood panels. Rajasthani window shutters work beautifully. Then use a matching window treatment on the two windows — probably simple curtain panels will look best. For the top-hung window, the curtains must come below the shutters or wood panels

 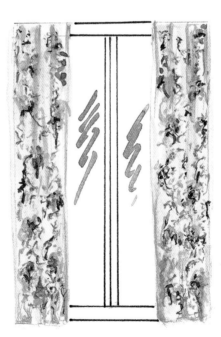

Renderings by Sheryl Perry

which will now be level with the bottom of the sliding window. Make the curtains the same length.

Q. There are recessed spaces below the windows of our new flat. Should we hang full length curtains for a cover-up?

A. Why waste precious space? Have doors and shelves made to create extra storage cupboards. You can choose simple doors and paint them to match the walls to blend in or make them more interesting with louvered doors or those with fancier mouldings. In a child's bedroom, doors can be painted in an accent colour or laminated so you can wipe off grimy finger prints.

Q. What kind of window treatment is good for bay windows? I don't want the heavy look of drapes, but we need privacy.

A. Venetian blinds would be a perfect solution to your dilemma. You will get good coverage and lots of style. You can go for mini blinds or get a great new look with wider slats than what we've seen in many years, which are really more in proportion for bigger windows. Many new colours are around too, so there's something to suit any kind of colour scheme.

Q. How can I hide the ugly ventilation openings above the windows without blocking off the air flow?

A. A lean and clean window treatment works best for problems like this. Venetian or mini blinds are good because they can be tilted to hide the uglies and still let in the air. Get the made-to-measure kind so the ventilation openings and the bottom windows can be fitted separately for individual control.

Alternately, you can install up-to-date looking transoms that open from the top. Leave them bare. Cover the windows below with the latest — wood Venetian blinds with extra wide slats.

Q. What sort of window treatment will look good on short top-hung windows at the end of the corridor? For ventilation, they are always open.

A. Allow for maximum air flow by leaving the windows uncovered. If privacy is a concern, change to frosted glass panes. Paint window frame and the nearby door frames a great accent colour.

Why not give the area a decorator's touch by painting the whole corridor a couple of shades lighter than the frames. The space will be transferred from "doom and gloom" to smashing.

Q. Do you have any suggestions for handling the recessed windows with window seats in our son's bedroom and in the TV room?

A. Any kind of flat blind will work. Cover the blinds and window-seat cushions in matching fabric.

Q. Please advise a treatment for casement windows that will block strong sunlight during the day while we are at work but will allow a good air flow when we open the windows at night.

A. For daytime protection when you have the windows closed, I recommend that you have a sun blocking UV film applied to the inside of the windows. I did this on all the windows in one of our homes, and it made a big difference. Choose dark grey film to keep a natural look from the inside, which is not as noticeable from the outside as dark brown.

Then go for draw drapes suited to your decor. The rod should be mounted far enough from the window frame to keep the drapery panels well away from the open window.

Q. What's a nice, simple way to do a window in a child's room?

A. Choose a cheerful roller blind like this one by Luxaflex (*left photo on page 190*). It's an easy, functional treatment that works for both boys and girls.

Q. I love bright, flowery prints and want curtains like that for my living room, but the sofa set is a modern style and covered with a geometric fabric. Can I mix the two patterns?

A. No, the result would be too busy. While it's quite okay to mix patterned fabrics, the feeling must be the same, and they must blend with one another. Why not take your idea for floral curtains to the bedroom? You can have a duvet or bed cover made in a matching or coordinating fabric for a total look.

For the living room, make drapes in a solid colour selected from the geometric fabric on the sofa set. Border them with fabric in one of the other colours in the pattern. An unfussy window treatment will work best with your modern furniture.

Q. What is the best way to care for my new drapes?

A. Always ask if fabrics are washable or must be dry-cleaned when you choose them. Keep a file with notes about their care. In between serious cleaning, you should vacuum the drapes every week or two, using the special attachment on your vacuum cleaner.

Many lace and net curtains can be washed, and they should be done frequently, soaking first in cold water with a mild detergent. Then they should be handwashed, or machine washed on the gentle setting in cold water to be safe. To prevent creasing, hang dripping wet on a line and let them dry naturally. While they are still damp, gently stretch them into shape.

Be sure to remove the hooks and other hardware before washing or dry-cleaning.

Q. How can I do an arched window? Everyone wants to put up a straight rod and draw drapes that will hide the arches.

A. All you need is a custom-made curved rod. From that you can hang two panels of your choice that are held back with cording for light and released to allow the panels to close for privacy. For something special, you can go a bit further with this treatment like Rosalie Chidwick did. She used a patterned, semi-sheer fabric held back with tasselled cords. Underneath, a gorgeous Roman blind is mounted a third of the way down from the top of the window. The delicate design that frames the window was stencilled on by Rosalie (*right photo on page 190*).

Q. I have a window that's got a sharp angle at the top. Regular curtains look silly and ruin the modern architectural features of our flat. How can I cover this window for privacy?

A. Custom-fitted vertical blinds work very well for angled shapes. They come in a variety of colours that suit most any scheme and are especially compatible with modern and contemporary themes. ❧

MORE PROBLEM WINDOWS

Most homes have a few difficult windows that are likely to cause treatment tantrums. Here's how to solve those irritating problems and get some stunning new looks too.

▲ *Photo courtesy of Luxaflex*
and Window Furnishing India Pvt. Ltd.

Arched Privacy ▶
This total look for an arched
window was designed by
professional designer Rosalie
Chidwick for her flat.
Photo by Pallon Daruwala ❧

Aging, but nicely shaped window frames can be left to stand alone when privacy and strong sun are not a problem. It's the new streamlined way to show off attractive architecture. Refinish tacky looking frames or paint them to suit the colour scheme of the room.

Make narrow windows that seem too tall appear wider by extending the header past the window on both sides. Hang the curtains against the wall, exposing the whole window.

Deep set windows can be dressed from the outside of the recess like any other window. Fill in the recess with artificial plants — real ones are too messy and likely to dirty the curtains. Or go inside the recess and right to the window with blinds of your choice.

Wide, short windows grow taller by raising the top of the curtains well above the frame. Fill in the gap with deep pelmets or swags and go floor length with curtains that meet in the middle and tied back at the sides to visually reduce the width.

Bay windows take to flat blinds which have the added convenience of individual control. A single pelmet lends a unifying element to the bays. Soften, if you like, the look of mini blinds with a balloon-styled pelmet and panels hung on either side of the bay windows. Multiple windows get the same treatment without the option of side panels.

Side-by-side windows, even unmatched ones, are best treated as a single window with the pelmet placed at the top of the tallest window. When they are just too ugly, cover up the whole mess with Roman or festoon blinds that can be controlled separately. Make them the size of the larger window.

Odd shapes like half moons, rounds, slanted windows, and hexagons are easily covered with custom-made Duettes. Dress up regular windows in the same room with curtains using matching Duettes as an under-treatment for a put-together look.

Arched windows provide dramatic focal points and should be treated accordingly. When you can't leave them alone to show off their natural glory, go with the full treatment or a new, less complicated version with the same feeling. Small arched windows take to festoon blinds. Whichever way you go, show the shape of the window unless you just can't stand arches.

A single corner window that abuts a wall or closet can go with an asymmetric style and flat under-blinds. Or let the blinds stand alone if you prefer. A pair of corner windows should be treated the same way.

Glass sliding-doors get treated like any other expansive window with a few modifications to allow for opening and closing. Decorative poles and curtain rods should extend past the frames to keep curtains out of the way. It's best to go with a lightweight fabric that isn't too heavy to pull.

Different-sized windows that aren't on the same wall should be done up with matching fabrics in coordinating styles but shaped to suit their individual sizes. For example, use festoon blinds on small windows to go with a classic look on normal windows. Or tie back shorties to outfit small windows and go with the floor-length version on big windows. Put the under treatment on both windows or just one, depending upon your needs and wants.

CHAPTER 9

Essentials

INTRODUCTION

Floors, walls and lighting are functional elements that go into all buildings. In your home they become more than construction essentials though. Each one of them can be used to its fullest measure in creating the setting you want in your personal environment. Many different types, styles and materials are used these days, giving you much to choose from. And like all phases of decorating, it can be confusing. Take time to learn about flooring options and care, wall treatments and lighting techniques. Only then can you make informed decisions about what is best for your home and your lifestyle.

FLOORS

Since flooring will take a huge hunk out of your decorating budget, choosing the right one is a serious matter. It is also something you want to last a long time, so you should like it a lot.

While the purpose of a floor is purely functional, it is also an important decorating tool that should tie in with your decor and lifestyle. For example, if you go for a cosy country look and there are small children around the house, a warm-looking wood floor that is easy to wipe clean may be just the thing for you.

On the other hand, a dramatic hi-tech setting is good on black slate or ceramic tile. Classic designs go well on marble or granite. Tribal and regional decor really should go on terracotta tiling or wood floors.

Flooring can even make a tiny home appear more spacious when all the floors are covered with the same material. If you can't afford that, at least use the same colour throughout — something like off-white marble in the living room and matching ceramic tile for the kitchen and bathroom.❧

Q. We love the look of wood but is wooden flooring practical?

A. At one time not too long ago, wood was a common flooring material used all over the world simply because it was inexpensive and very serviceable. We are currently experiencing a resurgence in its popularity as people re-discover the practicality and versatility of wood flooring. It is a huge favourite in the United States right now and is being used in the most unlikely places like kitchens and bathrooms. Although much of the world may not be ready for that kind of revolutionary decorating, wood is still an appealing floor covering that can give you years of beauty and service.

Be sure it has been properly dried and sealed with at least two coats of clear polyurethane, leaving 24 hours drying time between coats. It's worth the wait because the surface then becomes as hard as ceramic tile and is just as easy to wipe clean.

The big worry is termites, so the wood must be treated before it is brought into the house. For insurance, you should engage a reliable pest control company to do regular inspections.

Wood flooring is getting more expensive as timber becomes scarcer, but there's nothing like the rich glow of wooden flooring to enhance most any setting.

Q. The theme of our new flat is north Indian which calls for the look of a natural wood floor. Pergo flooring seems to blend in well and suits our budget, but is it any good?

A. It certainly has its good points, and I can see why you want to use this type of product — the price is right and it gives you a choice of fashion finishes and colours.

The main drawback is that it's laminate on top of chip board which absorbs moisture. Water that gets between the cracks is soaked up and the flooring can buckle. It should be all right in dry climate-controlled areas such as bedrooms and studies that don't get too much traffic. But wet places like bathrooms aren't a good idea, neither are busy or messy areas that need a lot of washing.

On the other hand, it comes in planks and is very inexpensive so damaged areas are easily replaced.

Q. I crave parquet[1] flooring. How do I choose the right kind of quality and tone, and how do I care for it?

---

1. Parquet: flooring made of short strips or blocks of wood that form a pattern. Sometimes inlayed with different kinds or varying colours of wood or other materials.

A. Choosing a good quality is a bit tricky, and you need to do your homework. For starters, ask people you know about their experiences, and check out the yellow pages of the phone book for a list of sources.

This isn't a decision that can be made in a hurry, so take your time looking and talking to retailers. They will each try to push their products, but the final decision is between you and your designer or contractor.

Besides quality, you must carefully consider the various types of finishes and sealers. Some scratch very easily, so don't cut corners to save money.

The tone of the wood should be coordinated with the style and colour scheme of your home. For example, country and tribal can take a heavier feeling, contemporary can go lighter, and Mediterranean is usually better with a natural shade.

You must also think about the area rugs and upholstered furniture you're going to use. Parquet flooring already has a certain amount of pattern in the design so watch out that you don't get carried away with too many different patterns.

Usually, the best way to clean a wood floor is to dust or vacuum it first, then wipe with a damp mop. Some types of finishes need waxing and others don't. You will need to ask for particulars about your flooring from the retailer.

Q. We are stuck in the middle of decorating our new flat. We decided on wood parquet flooring for the bedrooms and study, but that's as far as we've got because we don't know what kind of flooring to use in the rest of the place. We're going for an open concept in a contemporary, sophisticated look with basically black furnishings, white granite dining and sofa tables, accessories in shades of gold.

A. Wood parquet flooring is great in a contemporary setting. So why not go further and cover the living room, dining room and kitchen floors with the same thing? Put down area rugs to define groupings and to protect heavily trafficked spots.

Use black slate on the bathrooms and balcony floors for a smart out-of-the-ordinary look. It's also easy to keep clean.

Q. What are the good and bad points of ceramic tile, marble and terrazzo[1] flooring? We are a working couple with two active kids and need something that's easy to keep clean.

A. All three materials have some things in common: a hard unyielding surface which means they are hard on your feet, legs and back when you spend long hours doing cleaning, cooking and ironing. But they are good-looking, cool and relatively easy to keep clean.

These beautiful mosaic designs are wonderful inside or out. They look like a permanent throw rug and are very effective in foyers. Photo by author

---

1. Terrazzo: a mosaic material made of chips of broken stone, usually marble, and mixed with concrete.

So many different types of tiles are available these days that there's something to suit every taste, decor and pocketbook. Whether it's imported or local material, tile is a popular choice because it's the no-fuss way to go. However, tiles will break if something very heavy is dropped on them, so be sure to buy extra tiles for replacements.

If you're thinking of using tiles, talk to a decorator at one of the up-market stores for some smashing new ideas. Otherwise, tile floors can look very ordinary.

Buy the best quality you can afford. Ceramic tile is glazed which prevents any stain from soaking in, and those with textured surfaces give added protection against slipping. Homogeneous tiles have colour all the way through so small chips don't show up. But this kind of tile is porous. Dirt and spills seep down into the tile and stain it permanently. Ceramic tiles are priced from cheap to over the top for imported designer tiles.

Marble flooring is quite popular in India and is well suited to the climate. It's easy to maintain, but be careful with it because marble is porous and will stain. And since it's a fairly soft material, it is easily damaged. Like ceramic tile, the price range for marble varies greatly between indigenous and imported varieties. Granite is harder than marble and is often preferred because it doesn't stain or chip very easily. On the down side, there is not much variation in the natural colour, and some people find it too boring.

Terrazzo is a mosaic flooring composed of chips of broken stone, usually marble, and cement. It has a multi-coloured effect and can be rather busy. It is more durable than marble and, like ceramic tile, is stain and moisture resistant.

Q. What can I do about an orange juice stain on our light beige marble floor? I'm so upset. Even though I wiped it up immediately, a stain had already formed.

A. That's the big drawback to marble flooring. Accidents will happen and since it's a porous material, spills are instantly absorbed.

To remove stains from white or natural beige marble, soak paper towelling with straight bleach and apply it to the spot for several hours. Before trying this method, you absolutely must pretest your marble in a small unnoticeable area. Don't get hasty and make a costly mistake.

A sure-fire way to cover up the stain is to hide it — under a throw rug or a piece of furniture. Prevent future problems by using attractive washable rugs like cotton durries under the dining table and in areas where spills are most likely.

Q. I've chosen the wrong ceramic tile for my flooring. It stains easily and has an etched out design that collects dirt and grime.

A. Sounds like you've got a porous tile that soaks up spills. You need to have several coats of polyurethane applied. But first the tiles must be thoroughly cleaned. "Let your fingers do the walking" through the yellow pages to find tile companies that offer this service. Get several estimates.

After normal scrubbing, tiles with indented designs look bad because dirty mop water gets trapped in the grooves. To keep floors looking good, you need a vacuum floor scrubber that sucks up the mess as you go.

Q. The terracotta tile flooring on the balcony at our newly renovated flat is ruined. We think the contractor tried to clean it with a powerful liquid cement remover. What should I do about it?

A. Create a fuss over the damage and demand an explanation from the contractor. If you can prove he's responsible, he owes you a new floor. However, be prepared to get stuck with the problem.

Before you spend a lot of money hacking out the whole floor, here's a suggestion: chip out the damaged tiles and fill up the hole with concrete. Then create an up-to-date mosaic pattern by pressing in new ceramic tiles. Don't worry about varying sizes because the concrete itself becomes part of the new design.

Choose a Mediterranean-inspired peasant motif to tie in with an earthy feeling or maybe something in blue and white or even multicoloured tiles that have a hand-painted look will be terrific.

Q. We will be renovating our apartment soon. My husband likes terracotta very much and insists that it will make the kitchen look terrific. Is it difficult to maintain?

A. Terracotta clay tiles for kitchen flooring can present problems. Their uneven surface makes it difficult to level appliances and cabinets, often requiring an expert to get it right. Although a top quality sealer will prevent water and oil absorption, it tends to scratch very easily. Not the best choice for a busy, high-traffic area. Go for the look instead with terracotta-coloured ceramic tiles.

Q. We're interested in the natural look of slate. Does it make a good flooring?

A. Slate has an uneven surface that is good for garden paths, outside patios, balconies, and around swimming pools. It's also very handsome used in entrance halls and bathrooms. Otherwise, please be aware that it has an inherently uneven surface that is hard on feet and backs, making it impractical for kitchens.

Tip: To clean hard surfaces, wipe with plain water or a mild detergent. Use a minimum amount of water and dry off the floor when you finish. Too much water eventually ruins most kinds of flooring. To cover up scratches in wood, rub a matching shade of brown shoe polish into the scratch. For getting stains out of white marble, soak paper towelling with straight bleach and apply to stain for several hours. Resoak paper towels if necessary. This is not recommended for coloured marble. Natural beige is probably all right, but pretest to be sure. Don't make costly mistakes. Black marks made by shoes can be removed with a mixture of white spirit, water and detergent. To restore wood, stone and marble floors, polish and buff up with a clean cloth — but not too often. Otherwise, polish and wax will build up and make it dangerously slippery. Rub shoe polish of a matching colour on terracotta and quarry stone tile to cover white marks and scratches.

Q. Wall-to-wall carpeting seems easier to care for than bare floors — like vacuuming is enough and no scrubbing is necessary. Is this true?

A. On the contrary, caring for carpeting is more difficult and troublesome than hard surfaces. Wall-to-wall carpets eventually have to be professionally cleaned; they show wear and tear rather quickly, especially in heavily trafficked areas; and in this climate are subject to mildew, moulds and bugs unless you plan to run an air conditioner constantly. Bare floors are more cooling and practical with area rugs added for colour and textural accents to enhance the decor of any room. Small rugs are a good investment too, because you can take them with you when you move house and change them around from room to room when you get tired of them.

Of course, for pure luxury there is nothing to compare

with a beautiful Oriental rug in silk or wool. While expensive silk rugs and collectors' pieces should not be put in high-traffic areas, wool rugs are very durable and can go just about anywhere.

Q. How can I child-proof our new wall-to-wall carpet against dirt, sand and crumbs?

A. I hope the carpet is Scotch-Guarded to protect against mud and spills. If not, DIY! Just follow the easy directions on the can and spray the most vulnerable areas. Washable cotton throw-rugs are the answer for entrances. Practical, economical and available in many colours and patterns, they can enhance your decor. Buy some functional indoor-outdoor mats to use outside the entrances for wiping little feet — and big ones too.

Conquer crumbs and other messes by placing a cheap plastic tablecloth under the child's chair during meal and snack time.

Q. What kinds of rugs make good, easy-care area rugs?

A. Light-weight reversible cotton durries are good here since they are washable and can be turned over every week or two to guard against mildew. Another type that is especially suitable are flat-woven kilims with colourful geometric patterns, which can become the main focal point of an otherwise drab room.

Sisal or coir matting is inexpensive and makes a good-looking textured base for almost any style of decor, especially a natural or regional look. But these materials are not suitable for children's rooms because they are too prickly for little bare feet.

Tip: To care for carpets and rugs, vacuum them frequently, especially when they are put down in busy areas. Always vacuum them in one direction — with the nap, and be careful not to suck up the fringe. They will also need cleaning from time to time. This not only makes them look better, it gives them a longer life since ground-in dirt wears away the fibres. Small rugs that are hard to vacuum can be brushed softly, but do not brush the fringed edges as this destroys the fringe. Roll up rugs when you wash the floor because the edges of the rug absorb dirt from a wet mop or scrubbing cloth. At least once a week, check under rugs. If mildew is present, launder rugs that are washable; and place those that aren't washable in the sunshine, mildewed side up. If the floor seems damp, roll up the rugs and let the floor dry thoroughly before replacing them.

Q. We are interested in purchasing an Oriental carpet but don't know much about it. Can you please give us some pointers?

A. The term Oriental carpets usually refers to carpets that have roots in the Middle East and Asia. It's a broad subject and there's lots to learn about buying them. First of all, I have an important word of caution: do not assume that a salesman will give you totally reliable information — remember that his job is to sell the merchandise. Educate yourself on the subject before spending your hard-earned money. Visit the local libraries and book stores. Read everything you can find. It's always good to network with some serious collectors, most of whom are delighted to pass on their knowledge.

Talk to reputable, well-known carpet *dealers* (rather than salesmen). You can learn a lot from them when you know enough to ask the right questions and sift through the baloney. And finally, look and look and look. Your main objective should be to train your eye so you can trust your own judgement.

Before you go shopping, decide where the carpet will be used. Do you want a work of art, a wall decoration or a floor covering? Will it be used in a high-traffic area? If you need a serviceable wool rug for the entry way, don't let yourself get talked into buying a more delicate silk rug.

Vegetable dyes were used in antique wool and silk carpets. Ageing causes organic dyes to become soft and muted, which is considered an asset. Goat, camel and yak hair usually were not dyed, appearing in their natural colours. Modern carpets are made from a combination of durable synthetic and vegetable dyes that fade to paler shades of their original colour during the aging process. German aniline dyes were used at the beginning of this century and substituted for costly and difficult-to-produce vegetable dyes. Aniline dyes were intended for cotton and not suited to carpets and, therefore, deteriorated the quality of the carpets. Do not buy a carpet of this type.

To test for aniline dyes, moisten a piece of white cloth and run it over the carpet. If only a little of the colour comes off, it is okay. However, if a lot of colour rubs off, aniline dyes were used.

The warp (vertical) and weft (horizontal) form the base (or backing) of a carpet and can be seen at the base of the fringe on the ends of the carpet. Wool yarn is attached to the warp, knot by knot. After knots are bound to the warp, they are evenly cut with scissors. Sometimes at this stage the outline of the ornamentations are cut out. This process is called sculpting. Silk rugs are made in the same way as wool carpets, except each silk thread is skillfully cut to the required length immediately after it is secured to the warp.

Antique carpets were made from sheep's wool; goat, camel (soft and springy) and yak (coarse) hair; silk and precious metal. Silk should be hard and compressed. Inferior grades of silk produce a too-soft effect. Wool can be used to create any pile height whereas silk rugs usually have a flatter pile. The best grade of wool comes from the neck of young sheep. Silk and metal threads, with a high number of knots, create the finest, most defined patterns. Unfortunately, silk rugs are also the most fragile. Antique silk rugs should be used as wall hangings and new ones should be either hung or used in low-traffic areas.

New carpets are made of wool, silk, synthetics, and wool mixed with silk. Authentic Chinese rugs are never made of cotton but Japanese imitations of both Chinese and Persian carpets are frequently made of cotton or jute.

The quality of Oriental carpets is determined by the number of knots per square inch, material used and clarity of design. The higher the number of knots, the better the carpet. Surfaces will be hard and patterns will be well executed when the knots are very dense. Flip the carpets over to check the backs where the designs should be as clearly defined as from the fronts.

Traditional designs and colours are the safest investment. Today's well-crafted carpets are tomorrow's antiques. Stay away from trendy background colours (pink, green, turquoise, purple, and grey) unless you are willing to discard your carpet when it goes out of style.

Now silk carpets with Chinese adaptations of Persian motifs and colours, also known as fake Persians, are being made in China. These rugs are beautifully done and may be purchased for decorating purposes but should not be bought for investment.

Q. Are there differences between determining the quality of Indian and other Oriental rugs?

A. Not really. All rugs and carpets should lie flat on the floor, and the edges should be fairly straight. Fold the sides of the carpet over until they meet in the centre. If the ends are off more than one inch, it is too uneven and is undesirable.

Some irregularities in the designs are to be expected in handmade products. However, gross irregularities are not acceptable. Should you be especially attracted to a carpet that is flawed by gross irregularities in either (or both) size or design, a sizable reduction in price is presumed.

Carefully examine the back of the carpet. The design on a handmade product should be as well-defined on the back as it is on the surface, whereas the design on a machine-made carpet is less distinct. Wear, damage and repairs are more easily seen from the back than from the front. If evidence of repairs is found, check the carpet's surface. The value of the carpet is somewhat lowered when it has been repaired properly and greatly lowered when done badly.

Fringes found at two ends of a carpet are the ends of the warp on which the article is woven. On a machine-made carpet the fringe is attached, and machine stitching is apparent.

Test the material. Remove a thread and untwist it with your fingers. Then try to twist it back to its original shape. If the thread was twisted by hand, it will return to its proper position. If the thread was machine twisted, it will not. The next test is to verify the material. A thread must be burned. Cotton, wool, hair, and silk each burn in a completely different fashion and each have a distinctly different odour.

Cotton will burn all the way down the thread. Silk and wool do not, but silk has a stronger odour than wool. Polyester thread melts. When analysing a silk rug, several threads from different areas should be tested to be sure the silk is not mixed with another material.

A wool carpet should not have a high sheen. If it does, it has probably been chemically treated and should not be purchased. Chemicals shorten the life of the carpet, and it will begin to show wear after only 10 to 15 years — a short time when one expects it to last for generations.

Finally, obtain a written, money-back guarantee from the seller stating the material, type of dye and number of lines per linear foot. In the case of antique and used carpets, the age should be stated. Guarantees are not usually provided at auctions.

Q. How do I take care of our beautiful new Indian carpet?

A. Technically all rugs should be cared for in the same way. Vacuum wool carpets, always moving the vacuum cleaner with the nap — never against the nap. Once a week, turn the carpet over and thoroughly vacuum the back. Do not vacuum or brush the fringe because vacuuming breaks it and brushing untwists it. It's important to watch the maids! They love to brush fringe and must be strictly warned against doing so.

Take small silk rugs and wool carpets outside for a good shaking about once a week. To thoroughly dry out rugs and carpets, preventing mould, mildew and dry rot, lay rugs and carpets — knot side up — in the sun for three to four hours. Then, turn them right side up for not longer than one hour. Otherwise, rugs and carpets should be protected from direct sunlight to prevent fading.

When the weight of heavy furniture has compressed the pile of a wool carpet, use an ordinary dinner fork to gently rake the pile backwards to lift it again. Rotate the carpet occasionally or rearrange the furniture to vary the weight distribution and traffic pattern.

Always ask the dealer about cleaning when you purchase the carpet. Inquire about the colour fastness of the dyes and, of course, the type of materials used to make the carpet.

The following cleaning suggestions are only for new wool carpets and should be undertaken with great caution in cases of emergency.

Small spills should be absorbed immediately with generous amounts of white paper towels. Press hard until the spot is completely dry because, otherwise, dirt will collect there and leave a spot.

To clean stubborn spots, dip a piece of white terry-cloth towelling in plain water and rub in a circular motion. Then smooth down the nap and pat dry.

Urine can cause irreparable damage. However, if Puppy has an accident on a new wool carpet, quick action may save it. Absorb the urine immediately with white paper or terry-cloth towelling. Next, pour plain water on the spot to dilute the urine. Repeat the drying process. Then sniff the spot. If any of the odour remains, start over and keep working until all of the evidence is gone.

Avoid using over-the-counter dry-cleaning products on Oriental carpets — antique, new, silk, or wool. They contain chemicals that may be harmful to the colour and materials. Soiled carpets should be professionally dry-cleaned.

Your new rug will last for many years, and even generations, if cared for properly. Orientals require a certain amount of attention, but your investment is worth it.

WALLS

There's more to walls these days than slapping on another coat of paint. Plain-looking walls in the same boring colours don't work anymore. Everybody's into lots of colour, different textures and faux finishes. Popular wall treatments such as sponging and ragging add interest, texture and dimension to a room. The techniques can take from one to three or more colours for lots of flexibility. Different looks from rustic to highly sophisticated are achieved with various colour combinations and application processes (*photo on page 202*). Walls have more detail without using wall-paper which inevitably causes problems in this climate. Most decorators agree that texturing is ideal for old places where the wall surfaces are uneven because it helps to cover up the imperfections. Dragging and stippling are special techniques for doors, trims, mouldings, and cabinets that give wonderful antiqued and distressed finishes.

These sophisticated treatments are done both by professionals who specialise in faux finishes and by amateur DIY types, trying their hand at it for the first time. There are several how-to books out on the subject and some paint companies have all the paraphernalia necessary to do the job — all that's required from you is patience and lots of practice. As with most things you try for the first time, start off with small projects.

Tip: If you don't have mouldings at the top of your walls, hand-stencilling and wallpaper borders that complement or coordinate with the walls are good to control sponging and ragging effects.

Q. What can we do to the walls that will improve the atmosphere in a couple of very small and gloomy rooms?

A. Some designers love to create drama with dark or strong colours in small rooms with poor lighting. I've seen clear red and hunter green used in small studies, deep lavender in a small bedroom, and navy and midnight blues for tiny dining rooms. All of the effects were quite smashing. Personally, I think you have a great opportunity to try your hand at sponge painting. A two- or three-colour process will give the walls added dimension and make these boring rooms the centres of attention.

Q. I am interested in doing black walls in my flat with black and white photos for high-drama wall decorations. Is this too over the top, and will I get tired of it?

A. My personal opinion is that you can do whatever you want to if it's only paint, which is so easy to change when you want a different look or mood. However, some decorators stress caution when using black. They advise black textured walls for an interesting dining room, study and a bachelor's bedroom. But they don't think that it is suitable for the general type of living room. I have to agree that a black living room should be furnished carefully. And I've seen it done with great success — flat black walls, white slip-covered furniture and white tile floors. A softer look is camel coloured slip covers on a beige floor.

On the safe side, black is an exciting colour for accents such as area rugs and picture rails. Black accents are good with bluish pinks, emerald greens and yellows into salmons. It's not good when black overpowers the colour it's supposed to be complementing and becomes the dominating colour.

Q. Are there any absolutely taboo colours that should never be used?

A. Mustard yellow for bedrooms is a bad choice. Ugh. Too flashy and not very restful. Colonial brown is too dark and muddy to use on the interior, and nobody likes it, except perhaps when it's used in a contemporary bathroom with stainless steel counters and basin.

As main colours, old gold and tan with lots of gold and orange tones are ugly. Glossy peach is sickening. Don't use

◄ Formally Faux
Multi layers of paint sponged onto these walls resulted in a textured wallpaper look. To achieve this effect, two shades of gold, dabs of raspberry, and tiny specks of metallic gold paint were sponged on over two base coats of dark blue. The most difficult part of this particular project was getting the right shades of the colours, especially the blue base.
Photo by Pallon Daruwala

it now — there are more lucent Mediterranean pinks and peaches to work with. Colours that are either too strong or too flat can become tiresome.

Q. I'm bored with the all-white walls throughout my house, and I want to paint the crown mouldings in decorator colours to liven up the place. Is it better to use a glossy paint or a matt finish to go with the walls?

A. Good for you! I applaud this plucky approach for getting a new look. But why not go one step further to include the woodwork plus the door and window frames? Pick colours that coordinate with your decor in slightly darker shades to the setting without jarring the senses. Use an oil based high gloss — it adds more pizzazz and is easier to wipe clean.

Tip: Painting is a surefire way to spruce up tired walls. Get brave and try out new colours that suit your personality. Stay away from sickly greens and greenish-yellows which turn your skin tone green. Soft peachy colours are the most flattering. Stark white can be very drama or boring depending on the rest of the decor. Whites with a hint of pink are better.

Q. For something new and different, I want to sponge paint the doors on our kitchen cabinets. But I'm afraid I'll end up with a mess when I wash them. Won't the paint come off too?

A. Repeated washing will eventually wear down water-based latex paint. It's better to use oil based-paints every-where that needs frequent wiping. Oil based paints are more difficult to work with than water-based, so I suggest that you practice with them before you try sponging your cabinet doors.

Q. What's a way to brighten up a very boring wall in our eating area? The wall isn't in very good condition either.

A. To spruce up a drab ugly wall, frame some items and create an interesting grouping that relates to the setting. These days you can frame anything and hang it any old way. Choose items that will work into the theme surrounding your eating area — kitchen, dining/living room combo or dining room. Or vice versa: you can establish the theme with the grouping and carry it throughout the area.

Old rules about where and how to hang pictures are out of the window. Now you can put them where you want to, even next to the floor which works especially well when you have a big boo-boo on the wall to cover up. Refer to *Chapter10* for details on arranging a wall grouping.

Another option is to hand-stencil the wall with a cheerful design like that in the ***photo on right.*** While this wall is actually on a balcony that is arranged for alfresco dining, the idea is so flexible that it will work just as well in an indoor dining area.

Q. I'm thinking about wallpapering the living room myself to save money. Is it hard to do?

A. Wallpapering takes know-how, skill and patience to install properly. Mistakes are costly, and there is more to it than smearing glue on the back and slapping it on the wall. You need to know about things like plumb-lines, trimming out seams and matching patterns.

Get a good how-to book and read up on wallpapering techniques. You might as well learn to do it properly. I recommend that you practice a bit before you take on one of the public rooms. Start with something simple like a wallpaper border, and then do up a small room.

One more piece of advice — don't make a boring choice

Hiding the Flaws
Hand-stencilled designs hide the damage on this wall of Rosalie Chidwick's alfresco dining balcony. The same idea is most effective indoors as well as out. Photo by Rosalie Chidwick

such as a textured solid colour. You can get that look these days with paint finishes. Go for a pattern that will enhance your decor. You probably will need some help coordinating the wallpaper with other elements in the room. Don't use small prints in a large room. From afar, dainty patterns are not perceptible. Designs become indistinguishable from their backgrounds, and the effect is that of a solid colour. Consequently, any impact the prints were supposed to have is lost in space. Keep patterns and room size in proportion. The guidelines are easy: use large prints in big rooms and small prints in little rooms. Treat stripes in the same manner as prints. Remember that ceiling height affects the over-all size of a room. High ceilings give small rooms added dimension that allows more leeway in decorating.

Q. I think a dividing wall between the kitchen and the eating area is the best way to keep cooking odours and grease out of the rest of our home. However, that shuts out the natural light we get from the kitchen windows and makes the eating area feel boxy. What are my options?

A. Thanks to the revived popularity of glass blocks, you can let in the light which visually expands space and still keep rooms well defined. Since glass blocks work for both inside and outside walls, you can use them in a variety of ways.[1] (For different uses of glass blocks, refer to illustrations in *Chapters 3, 4 and 7.*) Another plus — they are easy to clean and never need painting.

A word of caution: use glass blocks in areas where complete privacy isn't necessary because although images are distorted,

you can see through them to some extent, especially at night when inside lights are on.

Q. The previous tenants left nail holes all over the walls. How can we repair the damage?

A. Fill the holes with plaster of paris which gives a smoother finish than concrete. Don't be in a hurry. First fill the holes, tapering off at the edges. Let it dry for several hours or preferably overnight. Repeat process because the material shrinks as it dries. Sometimes even a third application is necessary. Use sandpaper to buff off the rough parts. I have done this myself and made it work. And as the old saying goes, if I can do it, so can you.

Q. How can we decorate the dreary walls of our staircase landing? There is no window to dress and nothing distinguishing about the architecture.

A. Give the landing lots of eye appeal by creating a faux window with a scene of your choice such as a lovely garden, a seaside view, or whatever you like that looks so life-like you will want to walk up to it for a closer view. You can do this with either wallpaper murals, stencilled-on or hand-painted designs. Then hang a curtain around it or put an old window frame around the scene of your choice. Sometimes a window frame is painted on, but I think the real thing makes the whole idea more believable. Another effective treatment is to place Rajasthani-styled or old wooden shutters at the sides of the scene. If you aren't

---

1. If you live in an apartment, be sure to get permission from the proper authorities before making <u>any</u> structural changes. A glass-block wall is heavier than the normal interior wall, so the flooring and foundation must be able to handle the extra weight.

the DIY type or don't want the expense of hiring someone to create your view, you can use the window frame or shutter idea around a picture or a mirror.

These ideas are also great for the end of gloomy corridors. Not only are ordinary spots transformed, the areas seem bigger, brighter and infinitely more appealing.

Q. Please suggest something interesting for our daughter's bedroom. Wallpaper is not an option!

A. For something new and different that one never finds boring, paint clouds on the ceiling. I had it done in one of our own rooms, and I can't over-emphasize the pleasure the treatment gives us. In fact, as the light changes during the day, you can even imagine the clouds moving across the ceiling. The effect is beautiful at night too. When you're lying in bed gazing up at them, you feel like you're floating — very relaxing (***photo opposite***).❧

LIGHTING

Lighting is an important part of the decorating process. It's the mood-setting element that makes some rooms feel cosy and restful while other rooms feel bright and lively. You can easily create any environment to suit every situation, but you need to know how to do it the right way. Here are a few simple guidelines to get you going.

Generally for proper lighting, a small space that is less than 16 sq. metres (150 sq. ft.) needs a total of 200 incandescent or 100 fluorescent watts. That includes everything — ceiling lights, lamps and area work lights.

Average spaces up to 75 sq. metres (250 sq. ft.) need 300 incandescent or 150 fluorescent watts. Large spaces of more than 75 sq. metres (250 sq. ft.) need one incandescent watt or one-half fluorescent watt per one-tenth sq. metre (one sq. ft.) of space.

Obviously, you need about twice as many incandescent watts as fluorescent watts. But there are good and bad points about both kinds.

Incandescent bulbs are relatively inexpensive and cost less than fluorescent tubes. Incandescent lighting is more natural which makes rooms look more interesting as textures, forms and shadows are emphasized. Also there are no annoying flickers or humming noises. Best of all, they give off a warm colour that's flattering to skin tones.

Fluorescent tubes are cooler. They last about ten times longer than a regular incandescent light bulb and produce three to four times as much light. In addition, light is spread evenly around the room which is a big plus for kitchens. On the down side, the bluish colour makes us all look awful — so very unflattering to skin tones. And office workers who do a lot of paper work under fluorescent lighting sometimes complain of headaches, probably because of the flickering and colour distortion.

Most decorators hate fluorescent lights but, if you have to use them, go for the warm white[1] tubes. They are easier on the eyes because the light is more natural and definitely more flattering to skin tones. As the name implies, they give a softer illumination with an intensity that equals old-fashioned white tubes. Even business offices would do well to make the transition to soft-white lighting.

Drifting Clouds ▶
These lovely clouds floating across the ceiling is yet another way to apply a faux treatment. Photo by Pallon Daruwala❧

---

1. Warm white fluorescent tubes are also called soft white.

Never, but never, use fluorescent lighting in the living and dining rooms and don't even think about putting them in the bedroom. They do not create the proper ambience for these rooms. The effect is too commercial and, plainly speaking, quite tacky. ❧

Q. How do I know what kind of lighting we will need in our new home?

A. Think about what each room will be used for, where the furniture will be placed and then decide what areas need to be lit up. If there's going to be an activity in a fixed location like a reading or sewing corner, light that zone first. Activity areas should be brightly lit to avoid eye strain. You'll need 100 to 150 watts of light for close-up work like reading. Halogen lamps make great reading and desk lamps. Then do the rest of the room as needed, mixing ceiling and overhead lighting with table and floor lamps. Relaxation areas should be softly lit, so you should have dimmer switches installed for easy light control to create interesting effects.

The foyer or entrance way should be made inviting to create a warm welcome. Diffused lighting from ceiling or wall sconces and decorative lamps with pink incandescent bulbs will give a soft effect. Except for shaded lamps, light should be aimed upwards rather than downwards because you don't want beams of light blinding your guests.

In the dining area, the table should be emphasized but light shouldn't be glaring. Again, a dimmer switch is a must. For an intimate romantic touch, go for gobs of candles. You just can't overdo that kind of ambience.

Since your bedroom is your special get-away spot, make it as inviting as possible. It's easy to do with the right kind of lighting. Sometimes contractors don't put ceiling lights in bedrooms, which is a big mistake. You really need plenty of brightness here for everyday things like finding your clothes in drawers and wardrobes. To set the stage for romance, turn the lights on low and use floor lamps where you can to give dark corners a soft glow. Put several of the lamps on dimmers to increase your lighting options.

The kitchen needs to be extremely well-lit so you can see what you're doing — for convenience and for safety. You have to be able to see what you are chopping so you don't mistake your fingers for a carrot! You can't do without ceiling lights here. Ceiling mounted eyeball spots are good solutions. For the best way to light up work areas, mount lights under the top cabinets that shine down on counter tops. Other work spaces like the stove and sink also need to be brightly lit.

Good overall lighting is needed in the bathroom for shaving and putting on makeup. Natural daylight is the best, so you'll want to use artificial lighting that looks like the real thing. For that effect nothing can beat good old-fashioned incandescent light bulbs well placed over the mirror. Not so long ago theatrical strip lighting seemed the perfect solution for putting on makeup. Thankfully their popularity has waned. They really are overkill, using an enormous amount of electricity to power hundreds of watts and putting out enough heat to give you a sunburn.

Porch steps, patios and driveways should be well lit for safety so you don't trip on something in the dark. You need down lights so you can see where your feet are. You need lights for security also, but that's a different kind of lighting. It doesn't have to be as bright and should light up doorways rather than walkways.

Q. What is the best way to choose a good lamp?

A. Don't buy a lamp just because it's pretty unless you're looking for something decorative. Try it out first by having the sales clerk put it on a side table for you so you can check out the height and to see how wide a beam the shade allows.

Wall hung swing-arm lamps are versatile and convenient.

Since they are adjustable, you can aim the light any direction you want. Although they are usually brass, the styling ranges from traditional to contemporary so they look good any place, including on either side of the bed, at each end of a two-seater sofa, next to a chair, and over a desk.

Standing floor lamps are attractive and practical because they can be moved around as needed. Another plus is that they don't take up valuable table space.

Q. When we renovate our flat, I'm thinking about installing lights in the wardrobes. Is that a good idea?

A. Yes, it's a good idea because it's especially helpful for finding clothes and shoes in usually dark areas. Some people like to use bulbs in wardrobes to dry them out, which keeps everything smelling fresher and prevents mildew. However, from personal experience I offer a word of caution — clothing fades when it's exposed to incandescent lighting that stays on for any length of time. It's happened to me! Therefore be sure to install a switch in the door so the light only comes on when the door is opened and goes off automatically when the door is shut. Check it frequently to see that it's working properly.

Q. My room is painted lily-white with pale grey floor tiles. It looks especially glaring with my white fluorescent lighting. Without repainting the walls, how can such a colour scheme be softened?

A. It's very simple and cheap to solve this problem. To mellow out things, just tone down the lighting by changing the white fluorescent tube to a warm white. The room instantly takes on a soft glow that's easier on the eyes and more complimentary to skin tones.

Kill the glare that bounces off the floor tiles by getting some inexpensive throw rugs to scatter around. Pick a colour to coordinate with your bedding to tie things together.

Q. I've heard that you can change the way a room looks with different lighting techniques. How is that done?

A. It's a decorating trick called mood lighting that is fairly simple to achieve. By controlling the lighting in a room, the look and feeling can go from cosy to party time or whatever the occasion calls for. For example, to get a soft and cosy look, which is great for bedrooms, lamp light the room with frosted incandescent bulbs that are not over 60 watts each. For the ultimate, use soft pink light bulbs, which make everybody look great. If you can't find pink, don't get creative because other colours don't work. Blue will makes people ghosty-looking and creepy, and yellow is just plain awful.

The correct alternative to pink bulbs is to have the lamp shades lined with a pale pink fabric. Trust me, it's worth the trouble.

For the most charming atmosphere, there's nothing like candlelight. A candlelit dinner for two creates a lovely setting that also works for a small, intimate dinner party. Actually, candles create a special effect that softens everybody's mood, so they should always be used at the table. During family dinners, you will find the kids respond as well and behave better in the subdued setting. I even use lots of candles and dim lighting for corporate dinner guests because people seem to relax and enjoy themselves more.

A party-time atmosphere calls for plenty of bright, festive lights. Not the kind that shines in your face, though. If you have adjustable lights like eyeball spots, aim them at plants, decorative objects and wall groupings to create the effect of indirect lighting.❧

CHAPTER 10

Decorating Tools

INTRODUCTION

In the end, the success of every decorating project depends upon the finishing touches; those extra things that are added to every room to make it complete — after the workers are gone. The most beautiful walls and the loveliest furniture cannot stand alone. They need help.

Now is the time to bring in the elements that say, "This is our *home*." And what are those secret ingredients which add the warmth and satisfaction that turn a house into a home? One word: accessories. Accessories come in many forms — wall hangings, photographs, throw pillows, table displays, collections, and even slipcovers, to name a few. It is the way in which these things are integrated that determines the success of a room. Not only must each element be able to stand alone, it must also complement the other elements in the room. That makes the process of accessorising sound more difficult than it is.

The idea is to accessorise with those material possessions which you love, those that give you pleasure. This chapter will teach you about framing your favourite photographs and art, how to hang them, how to display your collectibles, and how to add those special touches. You will find that some trial and error may be necessary to get it right, but you will know when it is. The results will be infinitely satisfying.

Accented Entry
Warm wood, textiles and terracotta accessories that Maureen Berlin arranged in her entry way set the mood
for the regional decor that flows throughout the flat. Photo by Pallon Daruwala ❧

ACCESSORIES

Q. I'm crazy about my Italian ultra-modern furniture but need help with accessories. I want to enhance the look without getting too sterile. Can you suggest something interesting and unusual?

A. The best way to emphasise something is to contrast it. Use trendy Balinese, or closer to home, tribal pieces. You can use lamps, statues, candlesticks, vases, baskets, masks, and spears for the wall, and tribal rugs for the wall or the floor. Be careful, though — don't overdo. A few unique pieces are enough. Ultra mod doesn't need much accessorising.

Q. I like strong African accent pieces all over the place, but I can't go with the raw heavy furniture that decorators seem to be showing with it. Isn't there something softer looking?

A. Yes, you can combine powerful African pieces and lighter weight furniture but nothing delicate or cutesy. Mix it up with natural-looking wicker, cane and wood pieces. Just keep the total picture in mind and don't let the furniture overpower the room.

Pull everything together with fabrics that complement the African motif. For upholstery, throw pillows and drapes, a fabric with a tribal or Oriental feeling will be most effective. Think earth tones with splotches of brightness and lots of green. Avoid washed-out colours and sickly pastels — they don't work in with a rugged look.

Tip: Don't over-accessorise with knick-knacks. Interesting pieces lose their importance when there are too many of them. Anyway, they are hard to keep clean and make rooms appear cluttered. Do keep accumulated treasures in a glass cabinet where they can be exhibited properly as a collection. An alternative is to display a few pieces and store the rest.

Then, from time-to-time, rotate them which will create a continuing interest in the collection.

Q. We have just repainted the interior of our house and made a few decorating changes. Now our furniture doesn't look right with the new decor. Can you suggest something that will make it fit in?

A. For quick make-overs, use slipcovers over the old coverings to make furniture look new and different. It is also a great everyday way to protect expensive pieces when little kids are around to mess things up and to update tired or boring furniture.

You can create a distinct decorating scheme by slip-covering sofas and chairs with a variety of interesting fabrics, some of which are very cheap. Whether you go for informal slipcovers, casual throws or more formal fitted covers, nothing could be easier or more serviceable. You can get any look from country to romantic to contemporary depending on the style and choice of fabric. Any kind of full-bodied material will do. For a casual feeling, go with canvas or muslin. Chintzes are good for those incurable romantics. Be sure to use a lining with thinner fabrics so they won't slide around.

Make coverings out of a washable fabric so they're easy to maintain and always look spiffy. Wash fabric in cold water (and iron it) before you take it to the sewer to reduce fading and shrinking.

This made-to-measure slipcover for a desk chair was sewn out of cheap cotton ticking, lined with plain white fabric to give it some extra body (*left, page 214*). It's an informal look that works for dressing up an ugly chair as well as ordinary folding chairs. Or you can go all out for those special occasions and use slipcovers on dining room chairs to match your decorations and colour schemes.

Sometimes stitching isn't even necessary — just a little ingenuity as I discovered when I decided our bedroom needed a reading corner, and I had run out of furniture. What I did have were a couple of old chairs and some extra bed linen. So I created an armless two-seater by pushing the two chairs together and giving them a quick fix (*right, below*). Two pillow covers were slipped over the backs of the chairs. Then, a flat twin-sized sheet was spread over the seats, wrapped around the corners and pinned in the back.

This simple style will work any place. Some flowered pillows tied with inexpensive tassels finished off the look that is smart enough for any casual setting.

Q. What can I do with a beautiful piece of tapestry that I bought? It's too pretty to hide in a drawer.

A. Have it mounted on a strip of wood or a rod so the tapestry can be hung. Refer to the ***photograph opposite*** to see how it's done. The piece must be held firmly and evenly across the top.

The textures and colours in tapestries, textiles and rugs make them excellent wall decorations. They also are very good coverups on walls that are not in very good condition.

Designed and photographed by the author ❧

Designed and photographed by the author ❧

Q. How can I decorate for special occasions like Christmas, birthday parties and New Years without spending a fortune on accessorising?

A. Along the way I have learned a few tricks. (1) Anything red looks like more because it is a stand-out colour and visually takes up space. So put red candles and big red bows everywhere. (2) Brass animals and stuffed toys such as dressed-up teddy bears make great decorations and add a touch of whimsy. (3) Use everyday things in unusual ways, especially

Standing Tall
Joan Griffes hung a huge tapestry in her living room that was most effective in softening the stark, white walls of her flat. Photo by Pallon Daruwala ૐ

Homemade Accessories
These delightful Christmas sentries flanking the front door of Carol Ratcliff's home were made by her. The inexpensive materials used to craft them are common clay pots and paint. Rendering by Sheryl Perry ૐ

when doing up table decorations. Plants, real or artificial, work as long-lasting centre pieces; bright coloured saris make beautiful tablecloths and Christmas tree skirting. (**Refer to Table Dressing in Chapter 3.**)

Another way to save money on temporary accessories is to make some of the items yourself, using inexpensive materials. A charming example of homemade items is shown on the **page 215,** in the rendering of Carol Ratcliff's decorated front door.

Tip: Artificial is the user-friendly way to accessorise for special events. The beauty of using faux materials is that they can be reused — over and over. I always buy materials, including silk flowers, that take well to spray paint so I can change things to work in with different theme decorations and new colour schemes.

PHOTOS AND ART

Q. Is it okay to hang contemporary art in a room that has a strong regional flavour?

A. Most certainly. It's totally amazing how the new blends with the old, whether it's new art and old furniture or new furniture and old art. While there are very few rules about what goes with what, there are lots of conflicting opinions. That's why the whole subject boils down to a matter of personal taste and judgement.

May Kottukapally-Demann's living room (**photo opposite**) is a wonderful example of the old and the new. She mixed bold contemporary paintings by the famous Indian artist Adimoolan with her mostly Rajasthani decor. The room is a riot of bright colours but the large paintings are the focal point[1], and the furnishings fall away into the back-ground.

Q. I have been to some photo exhibitions and loved what I've seen. Some of them are very expensive, though, and I'm wondering if they are worth the money?

A. Photography has become a fine art (**photo on page 218**). Many photographers are artists in their own right, and camera equipment and film processing techniques are so advanced that the finished product rivals oil paintings. As the art world recognised and honoured photography as an art form, interest among collectors and eventually the general public grew. It may seem expensive until one accepts the fact that you are purchasing original art — not a snapshot.

Professional photographer Pallon Daruwala's advice for buying fine art photographs is, "Always buy something you like and never spend more than you can afford." He goes on to offer these useful buying tips:

Check out the overall condition of the photograph. In most cases the art work should be in pristine condition. But there are exceptions that should not be passed up. When in doubt, ask.

When buying an older photograph, look for signs of abuse such as water stains, cracks and bends in the paper. If something doesn't look right, question it.

Pallon further cautions that you must remember these photographs are precious objects of art and to treat them accordingly to ensure your continued enjoyment of the piece and to protect your investment.

Q. The picture I want to hang in the dining room is too small

---

1. Focal point: something important in the room on which your eyes focus.

A Smooth Blend
The traditional-styled furniture is low, and the paintings are hung at eye level on a large expanse of stark-white wall for maximum effect in May Kottukapally-Demann's living room. The perfect placement lowers the ceiling and proportions the room, which further substantiates my motto: if it looks right and feels right, then it probably is right. Photo by Pallon Daruwala

Fine Art Photography
Photo by Pallon Daruwala ❧

for the wall. How can I solve this problem?

A. You can cover a big wall space by enlarging the picture you want to hang with an over-sized mounting treatment. The picture will grow to the size you need. I speak from experience, so I know this works. I mounted a piece of intricately designed blue and white fabric with triple mats to make it big enough to hang over a bed. The fabric is only 35.5 x 46 cms (14 x 18 ins.); the first mat next to the fabric is white and is 2.5 cms (1 in.) wide; next is a tiny navy-blue mat, 5 mm (one-eighth in.) wide; the third mat is white and is 10 cms (4 ins.) wide; the frame is a narrow, navy-blue enamel. The picture grew to 64 x 76.5 cms (25 x 30 ins.) and is smashing on a stark, white wall.

Q. Any ideas how I can decorate the corridor leading to the bedrooms? It's narrow and quite dim.

A. For starters, hang a mirror or a large picture on the wall at the end of the corridor. Put a narrow table or chest with a small lamp under it. This immediately brightens up the area and creates an interesting focal point that makes the hall seem shorter.

Decorate the walls with items that have details — something that you have to get up close to see clearly. Go for squarish frames or frames that are slightly taller than they are wide. Vertical oval shapes are good, too.

For an excellent example of how something terrific can be made out of an ordinary corridor, found in almost every home, refer to the ***photo on page 220*** for another example of the creative wizardry of Robert Mathis.

Framing

Q. What kinds of things can I frame, and how should they be done?

A. You can frame anything from original oils and watercolours to museum posters or cheap copies, a unique tapestry, an antique Chinese collar, pot shards, plates and bowls, certificates and diplomas, a treasured photograph of your grandmother and even newspaper clippings — the list is endless. Here are some guidelines — the operative word is *guidelines* because there are always exceptions.

Oil paintings should be rather plainly framed. In my humble opinion, a work of art should stand alone. If it has to depend upon the frame to bring out certain colours, the painting is not very substantial. Some experts say that certain canvases should be left "raw" and not framed at all. Sometimes the artist will even paint the sides of the canvas when it is intended to be hung without a frame. Oils literally must breathe. This means it is never covered with glass and never has a backing. Keep the framing technique modest. Do not select a frame that will compete with the painting.

Water colours and expensive prints must be sealed to protect against moisture. They should be mounted on acid-free paper (100% free of chemicals to prevent mildew) and covered with glass. Usually a mat is used to give the picture breathing space (literally and visually) and to raise the glass away from the picture so it will not stick to the glass.

Tapestries and other textiles are treated in different ways depending upon the item, but they are usually always put on a stretcher. Sometimes intricately embroidered pieces are handsewn onto a silk backing as well, with or without over-mats. However, if mats are not used, spacers must be inserted to lift the glass away from the fabric. Sometimes tapestries and textiles are not put under glass and mats — just stretched, with or without frames. For example, if the piece is sturdy and already decorative, stay simple. Have it put on a stretcher and hang without a frame. Glass and acid-free backings are not necessary either because stretched fabrics that are left open have better ventilation and are not so susceptible to humidity. Air circulation is critical to prevent mildew.

Awesome Ending
Smashing cinnabar walls decorate an otherwise nondescript corridor in Robert Mathis's flat. The lighted painting and decorative chest make an intriguing focal point. Photo by Pallon Daruwala

Sepia photos do not require coloured mats. They are more attractive and their antiquity is better enhanced with neutral fabric mats to match the subtleness and texture of sepia. Some good framing choices are antique gold (duller, warmer and browner than bright gold), muted tortoise-shell and beryl or cherry wood. Frames in warm brownish colours to match the sepia tones of the photos are important.

Black and white photos can be done without mats, but spacers must be inserted for air circulation. To make photos appear larger than they are, use off-white or grey mats. Silver-leafed wood (warmer than metal) or simple, black lacquer frames are best.

Colour photos are more versatile and subjective depending upon the look you want. Select mats and frames that match the most subtle colours in the photos rather than the most dominant colours to enhance the subject matter — not overwhelm it.

Tip: Professional photographer Pallon Daruwala's advice for framing fine art photographs is equally applicable to all photos. He says, "Never let the print surface touch the glass. Always use an over-mat or spacers designed especially for the frame you are using. When an over mat is not used, spacers keep the photograph from coming in contact with the glass."

Certificates and diplomas should be mounted simply. Usually mats are not needed because most of these items already have a wide margin. Choose silver or gold aluminium frames. Avoid boring, plain black frames — the look is too severe. However, these items are very personal and, therefore, personal taste should not be ignored. For example, my diploma is double framed in antique gold leaf with a silk mat. The total look, including the document, is old gold and cream — simple elegance which suits my taste. My husband's diploma is mounted without a mat. The sides of the frame are black and the front has a straight line of bright gold leaf that surrounds the document — very masculine. So, "To each his own."

Tip: Don't hang anything on a wall that is prone to dampness. Beware of water pipes hidden inside a wall because moisture tends to collect on the outside wall, especially in tropical climates. Frequently look behind wall hangings to check for mildew.

Q. Where should I go for good framing and what can I expect?

A. That depends upon what you are framing and what it is worth to you. If the item is an original work of art or a personal treasure, give it the best treatment. Some framers are artists in their own right and instinctively know how to enhance an already-good piece of art. When working with one of them, the best advice is to turn the piece over to them. This is what will happen....

Each piece is treated individually, and the end result is special. The framer looks at it, studies it and then knows what is needed. The experts will not ask you what colour are your walls and furniture, and where are you going to hang the finished product. They do not care! Shocking? Not at all, because this is the correct approach. The mounting[1] must match the picture, not its surroundings, to enhance the item's value and emphasise its importance. On the other hand, it should never overpower the item itself. Proper mounting can turn an ordinary picture into a real eye-catcher.

---

1. Mounting: a term used to describe the whole treatment of frame, mat(s) and backing(s).

But a bad job can kill most anything — at the very least, it will just hang there, unnoticed and doomed to obscurity.

Some framers take a slightly different approach. They ask the client whether they want a traditional or a modern look, and then recommend the proper mounting.

Prices can range anywhere from reasonable to wildly expensive. When dealing with the experts or anybody else, take the item in for a cost estimate. If the price is more than you want to pay, name a figure and ask what can be done for that amount.

If you just want to frame something ordinary — a print or a certificate, and you don't want to spend much, there are any number of local, down-market frame shops. Their only drawback is they are unimaginative, and you must design your own mounting. They also have a limited supply of mats and frames available.

Q. Which is better to use, regular or non-glare glass?

A. Artists and framers always tell you to use regular glass because non-glare glass hides the details. While I know this is true, I've had some debates with them over this. My objection to clear glass is that if something is hung where the artificial lighting causes such a glare that you can't see it anyway, why not use non-glare glass? They will usually concede the point — grudgingly. Normally, they will let you use non-glare glass on diplomas and certificates without too much argument.

Tip: Wall hangings should never be displayed where they are subjected to direct or indirect sunlight that damages and fades everything from oils to photographs and textiles.

Q. I have a lovely silver frame that was a gift, but the photo I want to put in it is too small. What can I do?

A. You can make a mat out of art paper that is the correct size for the frame. Cut the opening slightly smaller than the picture. Lay the mat face down on a flat surface, then lay the picture face down on top of it. Use clear tape to fix the back of the picture to the back side of the mat.

Q. What kind of pictures go in decorative photo frames? The pictures I've tried seem to clash with or diminish the impact of the frame. Or the frame swallows up the picture.

A. You're right. Many of these decorative frames can stand alone and don't even need a photo. But that isn't the idea, is it? So buy the frame to suit the picture — not the other way around. Rule of thumb: the objects in the picture must be larger than the decorations on the frame. A simple, un-complicated photo like a head shot can go in a busier frame. Group photos and landscapes take a plainer frame. Take your pictures and photos with you when you shop for frames.

Tip: Look in flea markets and junk shops for old frames. If they are in poor condition, strip off the old finish and re-stain or paint them. You can give them a gold or silver gilt look with metallic paint.

Q. We want to decorate our living room walls with pieces that look good, but expensive art is a luxury we can't afford now. Do you have a suggestion?

A. Buy cheap copies of lesser-known works (which no one will recognise) by famous artists and increase their importance with interesting — even elaborate, but not garish — mountings. Don't try this on a Mona Lisa copy, though, because you won't fool anyone.

Then make a project out of learning about up-and-coming local artists whose works are still affordable. Visit art galleries and go to art exhibitions. Talk to gallery owners regarding artists they promote. It's a fun way to start collecting original paintings, meet some interesting people, and broaden your knowledge of art all at the same time.❧

Arranging

Q. We want to hang some pictures and my husband and I can't agree on the right height. What are the rules for hanging pictures properly?

A. If the ceiling is 2 to 2.5 metres (7 to 8 ft.) high, hang major pieces at eye level. This means the centre of the picture should be at eye level or just slightly higher when you look at it from a standing position. When doing a grouping, the mid-point of the group should be at eye level. If the ceiling is 3.5 to 4.5 metres (12 to 15 ft.) high, you can hang very larger pieces higher. You can run groupings higher up the wall too.

Make paper patterns in the exact size of the pictures you want to hang. Then tape them to the wall. Leave them up for awhile to study the situation and move them about until you're satisfied. Once you can actually see the placement, I think you and your husband will agree on what's right for your walls.

Q. How should family photographs be displayed?

A. There's something especially meaningful about family photos but usually just to the people they belong to. Most are too personal to be shown off in the living room — at least that's what I used to think.

While I still frown on the idea of ordinary snap-shots hung on living-room walls, I've seen such beautifully framed photo collections displayed on both cloth-covered and bare wooden tables that I long to copy the idea. Indeed, small

and miniature standing frames are very vogue right now and look great on top of side tables and chests in any room (***photo on page 224***). Another good place for your little favourites is perched on a bedside table, close to you so you can really enjoy them.

Large photographs can be hung separately, medium-sized photos do well grouped together, and smaller pictures look best setting out rather than hanging.

Q. Where is the best place to hang our collection of random photos that includes some autographed pictures of well-known personalities?

A. Personal photos should be hung or placed in casual settings where it's easy to get close enough to see them. Corridors, studies, family rooms, and bedrooms are ideal places for displaying a whole wall of pictures. Amusing snapshots work in wacky places like the kitchen and the bathroom.

It is considered poor taste to display such personal items in a public area. Especially offensive are photos of family members shaking hands with famous people, an obvious form of bragging that is worse than name-dropping. A subtle way to display those famous-people photos is to group them on the wall outside the loo where guests are bound to eventually see them.

Tip: Do a collage of kiddy photos for the walls in the children's bedrooms. They love to see pictures of themselves, and it makes a colourful wall decoration.❧

Q. How can I pull together pictures in a grouping?

A. Although many decorators advise similar or even matching frames and mats, I group wall decorations according to subject matter and feeling. It isn't practical to

assume you are accidentally going to have matching frames, and it costs a bomb to have a whole grouping done up at once. Therefore, my way makes more sense. For example, while totally ignoring mountings, I grouped photographs of people's pets for one wall treatment and did a wall of certificates and diplomas for a study. Incidentally, I discovered that maps, both old and new, work in well with arrangements of the latter kind.

Q. What is the best way to arrange a wall grouping?

A. Here's the key to success: get out everything you want to hang and lay it on a flat surface — the floor will do. Let the creative juices flow and play with them.

You have to start somewhere, so pick out your favourites and put them where they can best be seen. Build onto them with the rest of the pictures to form the grouping. Keeping an overall balanced look is all that's really important and that's easy to do. For example, a big picture can be balanced out by stacking two or more smaller pictures on one side.

To keep from knocking unnecessary holes in the wall, cut dummy pictures out of old newspapers, making them the same size as the real ones. Tape the dummies on the wall to match the arrangement layed out on the floor. Now stand back and have a look. If the grouping is shaping up nicely, let it alone and just look at it for several days. If it's not good, rearrange the newspaper pieces.

To hang pictures use nails that are big enough to support whatever it is you are hanging. Heavy objects should be supported by two nails. Be sure the wire is strong and/or doubled.

◀ *Family Ties*
In the bay-window alcove of their living room,
Maureen Berlin displays a lovely grouping of family photos
on a handsome antique table. The Tiffany lamp provides
the light for easy viewing. Photo by Pallon Daruwala ❧

Q. I'm living in a rented apartment, and my landlord won't let me put hooks in the wall. How can I display my favourite landscapes?

A. The newest way to show off art is to stack it against the wall. This idea is being used far and wide — I've even seen it on the covers of some international decorating magazines. The floor is good for large pictures and big images that can be appreciated from a distance. Go too small and you'll have to crawl around on the floor to see them. Bookshelves work for smaller pieces. Decorative, free-standing easels are excellent platforms for showing off large and medium-sized canvases. The good thing about propping is you can change pictures around when you get tired of them without leaving big holes in the walls. ❧

COLLECTIONS AND DISPLAY

Q. We are a newly married couple with many lovely wedding gifts that should be displayed, but we've run out of places to put them. Our small apartment doesn't have a lot of space, and we can't afford an expensive display cabinet. What can we do?

A. Ah yes, a problem most of us face at one time or another. The solution is to use the walls and window ledges. Make display shelves out of lumber held up with brackets mounted to the walls. Paint them the same colour as the walls to blend in. For added interest, intersperse wood shelving with glass or plexiglass shelves. Window ledges are a natural for small objects and even books.

If space permits, buy an inexpensive see-through wall unit to double as a room divider between eating and living areas or kitchen and eating area.

You probably still won't have room for everything

Colour Conscious
The subtle use of colour pulls these mismatched elements together in a setting that's both comfortable and easy on the eyes. Styled and photographed by Rosalie Chidwick

so rotate your display pieces. Group similar items to create collections and prevent a hodgepodge look.

> *Tip: Glass shelving must be generously thick to hold the weight of the objects on display. There is no give to glass, and it will snap when stressed to the breaking point. Be sure to have the rims and sides finished off nicely so there are no sharp edges to cut yourself on.*

Q. We have collected an assortment of odds and ends that I want to work in with our furniture. How can I make everything look like it goes together?

A. One of the ways to make mismatched objects look as though they belong in the same room is to tie it up with a common colour like interior decorator Rosalie Chidwick did in her husband's study (**photo opposite**). She linked an eclectic collage of regional pieces, a primitive sculpture, contemporary art, and a wingback leather chair by subtly using the colour green. Starting with the oil painting in the upper right corner down to the throw pillow and rug, around to the green plant and old window shutter, Rosalie encircled the setting in green and used colour as the thread that pulls the arrangement together.

PLANTS AND CACTI

Q. What can we do to fill up our apartment? The rooms look so bare but we can't afford to buy anything else just yet.

A. Add plants to your rooms to decorate the bare spots. They make wonderful and affordable accessories. Place them in attractive but inexpensive containers that suit the feeling of the rooms. In a formal setting dressy-looking brass planters add a nice touch. For casual settings, ceramic or ornamental terracotta pots work well. Where you are trying to fill up larger areas, group together different kinds of indoor plants in different sizes. Medium-sized plants can go anywhere, on the floor next to a chair that looks lonely, at the end of a sofa, or in a corner. Small plants are good for bare-looking tables, shelves and window sills.

Besides their decorative value, plants are beneficial because they suck up carbon dioxide and give off oxygen for cleaner air indoors, counteracting the damage of pollution. So it is important to use real plants rather than artificial whenever it's practical. Please do protect surfaces from moisture though. Be sure to place non-porous receptacles under pots to catch excess water and to protect floors and furniture tops from dampness that comes from the bottoms of porous containers.

Q. I'd love to have houseplants but just can't get them to grow. What am I doing wrong?

A. Maybe they're homesick. It takes a little knowhow to choose the right plant for the right place. You can't plop them down just anywhere and expect them to be happy. Plants need a setting that is close to their natural habitat. So before you go shopping, decide where you want green things and check out the conditions.

For indoors and shady outdoor spots: some species of *Dracaena* do well in dark places. *Dieffenbachia, Schefflera, Spathiphyllum,* some species of *Calathea, Japanese Bamboo, Money Plant,* and *Rhapis* or *Lady Finger's Palm* are good. Spathiphyllum will put on unusual white flowers in a shady outdoors environment but not indoors.

Ficus can go indoors but it's rather finicky and wants lots of brightness and circulating air. When this plant is unhappy, leaves drop off like crazy. If that happens, try out different locations inside, move it to the balcony or set it in a shady spot in the garden.

Housebound
Indoors or shade only, please: (clockwise from 12 o'clock) Schefflera, Japanese Bamboo,
Spathiphyllum, Money Plant, Dieffenbachia, and Dracaena. Photo by the author

Yellow palms can come inside but not indefinitely. When they start drooping and looking unhappy, out they go for a stay in a friendlier setting.

Tip: Generally houseplants don't need watering more than two or three times a week. But if you can't be bothered or you're just plain forgetful, go easy on yourself with hydroponic plants — those that can be grown without soil. Just stick Money Plants, Japanese Bamboo, Dracaena and Dieffenbachia in vases of water and they will take root and grow.

Q. What are some really easy-care house plants?

A. There are several kinds of low-maintenance house-plants that will give you long-term enjoyment. One of the easiest to set around is cactus. It's such a hardy plant that it can even take extreme neglect. In fact, cactus can take almost anything except too much water. You only need to water it when it's completely dry, and most people don't bother with feeding and fertilising. If the cactus comes down with white spots, set it in the sun for awhile — the environment is too humid for it.

Some types of mini cactus have a kind of bright-coloured flower that make them very decorative. They look great sitting on the desk, dresser or shelf. They can go just about anywhere that's not too damp so don't put them in the bathroom. Near a window that gets full sun works just as well as a semi-dark corner with artificial lighting.

If you want a bigger houseplant to set on the floor but can't take a huge cactus with long, dangerous spikes, you can go for a Mother-in-law's Tongue. Also known as **Sansevieria**, it's a great decorating item for a spot that needs something tall — a bare corner, at the end of a sofa or in front of a post.

This plant is tough and thrives on neglect like cactus. It

The put-me-anywhere plant Sansevieria, also called Mother-in-law's Tongue. Photo by the author

takes very little water and will grow like crazy in places that don't get any sun or fresh air. An easy-care low maintenance plant, Mother-in-law's Tongue even does well in air conditioning and in rooms that get stifling hot when the a/c is turned off. Either way, it doesn't seem to care.

Tip: If you have children around the house, keep cactus plants out of reach. Even the mini variety have sharp spiny points that are dangerous to little ones.